Synthesis

Chris Thomas

Fortynine
publishing

First Published in Great Britain in 2011
by
Fortynine Publishing

A CIP catalogue record for this book
is available from the British Library

ISBN 978-0-9566696-1-2

Cover design by Fortynine Publishing
Cover image – The Sombrero galaxy (M104) photo taken by the Hubble Space Telescope

Fortynine Publishers
PO Box 49
Llandysul
SA44 4YU

Printed and bound in Wales by
Gomer Press, Llandysul, Ceredigion

Synthesis ('sinθisis) n. 1. the process of combining objects or ideas into a complete whole. 2. the combination produced by such a process.

Dedication

To Di

a light for when all other lights fail –
not bad for a fop!

I would also like to dedicate this book to

Laurence Gardner
and
Zecharia Sitchin

Both of these gentlemen died during 2010
and, whilst I disagree with much of what they wrote,
they nevertheless stimulated discussion and investigation
into subjects which opened the eyes of a great many people.
I wish both well on their journey to return home
to their places of soul origin.

Contents

List of Illustrations

Previously published books by Chris Thomas

The Journey Home
The Fool's First Steps
Planet Earth – The Universe's Experiment
The Universal Soul
The Human Soul
Project: Human Extinction – The Ultimate Conspiracy
(written with Dave Morgan)

The Annunaki Plan? or The Human Plan?
(published by Fortynine Publishing)

Books about healing co-written with Diane Baker

The Healing Book
Everything You Always Wanted To Know About Your Body But,
So Far Nobody's Been Able To Tell You

The Sequel To Everything

For details of how to order these books, please see the end of this book

Introduction

We are undergoing a process of change. A change so fundamental to our way of being that it is resulting in confusion and a lack of understanding of what this change is about or even why we are changing at all.

Even though there are many millions of solar systems throughout our Universe, ours is unique. Nowhere else within our Universe does "physical" life exist. The abundance of life and the variety of species that we share our Earth with outnumber the total number of species within this Universe. I will say that again – there are more forms of life on our Earth than the whole of the rest of this Universe combined.

This is what makes our solar system unique and the part that humans have had to play within the development of this universe is immeasurable.

We might feel like we are insignificant but, in reality, we have been of immense importance and continue to be of immense importance to the Universe as well as to the whole of Creation.

That might sound like it is not possible. After all, we are but insignificant beings living in a solar system located on the outside edge of nowhere. But, we have generally forgotten who and what we truly are and the role that we took to ourselves as this solar system began to develop life.

It is no good looking in our history books or even in religious texts to remember our true role. History books and religious texts only reveal an insignificant part of the real history that is ours. To remember who we *really* are, and our true history, we need to turn to the Akashic.

The Akashic is a word taken from ancient Sanskrit which means "Record". The Akashic records every single event that has ever occurred within this Universe from the very first second that this Universe first came into being. Needless to say there have been many events that have taken place and it is not possible to relate all of them. After all, our Universe has been in existence for over fourteen billion years and to tell the whole story would require an equal fourteen billion years to relate.

In my previous books, I have tried to tell the story contained within the Akashic, as related to human history, to try to explain many of the events and driving forces that have shaped our modern world. What I am attempting to do with this book is to try to tell the whole story of this Universe from the perspective of an over-view. In other words, the history of the Universe in a broad sweep rather than told with the details of every single event. This does not mean that there will only be the "edited highlights" without any detail, just that detail will be added where appropriate.

Many people are able to access the Akashic and the history it records. My own experience of accessing these records goes back to when I was of a very early age. I found that I could find the answers to questions asked by others even though I did not have enough experience of life. The answers, then, must have come from somewhere beyond me, beyond my own experiences and beyond my personal knowledge of the world. It took me a long time to find out just where these answers originated and that I was somehow "hard-wired" into that source. The source, of course, being the Akashic.

I have now actively worked within the Akashic for over thirty years and explored many aspects of human history and, by extension, Universal history.

There are some aspects of the Akashic which do need to be explained as there can be misunderstandings over just what the Akashic contains and how the Record is accessed.

To give an example of what I mean by this.

The country of Iraq can be described as the "cradle" of modern history. Northern Iraq was a region – locally known as Eden – where the origins of the traditions of the Old Testament arose (see Chapter Thirteen) whilst Southern Iraq is the region where a "scientific" approach was first attempted. It therefore follows that Iraq was very rich in artefacts which told the true story of early human history, many of which were contained in Iraq's museums and libraries.

When America and Britain invaded Iraq in the Second Gulf War in 2002, the chief aim of the invasion was to remove these artefacts to America where they could be kept hidden from the world.

So let us take the actions of one soldier to illustrate how the Akashic records events.

Soldiers were ordered to surround and protect all of the museums and libraries to ensure that the local inhabitants did not loot them whilst the specially briefed soldiers removed all of the records they were ordered to remove. Our soldier being one of these specialists – let us call him Joe Blogs.

Now Joe, along with his fellow specialists, enters a museum and carefully and systematically removes the items he has been detailed to remove. Once Joe has finished with one museum, or library, he moves on to the next, until he has completed his task.

The Akashic records that the invasion of Iraq was ordered as a cover for this systematic looting and that the looting was carried out by troops trained in this task. What it does *not* record is the names of the looters or the actions of individual troops as they went about their task.

This is what the Akashic does; it records events. What the Akashic does NOT do is to record the acts of individuals who took part in those events unless those individuals have a major role in how those events came about.

In other words, the lives of individuals, such as our soldier Joe Blogs, are not recorded within the Akashic.

However, Joe's part in the looting of Iraq is recorded within his own memories. The scientific viewpoint is that we record our memories in our brains, but this is not strictly true. Our brains record short-term memories; our long term memory is in our DNA.

DNA is considerably more than scientists understand. As far as science is concerned, we only use about 3 per cent of our DNA; the rest, 97 per cent, they consider to be "junk". In reality, this 97 per cent is our long term memory.

When we are conceived, we need about 25 per cent of our DNA to build the body of the foetus. When we are born, this percentage gradually drops until we arrive at puberty where we require 3 per cent of our DNA to maintain the adult body's systems, the remaining 22 per cent becomes our memory storage of our actions in this lifetime – this is why people who have illnesses such as Alzheimer's do not remember what they did last week but have full and clear memories of events that took place several years before. Alzheimer's disease destroys the connections within the brain which allow for short-term memory storage however, memories that have been transferred into our long-term storage, our DNA, are fully accessible.

The remaining 75 per cent of our DNA is our recorded memory of our previous lifetimes.

To re-cap: 3 per cent of our DNA is needed to maintain our physical bodies through our current lifetime. 22 per cent of our DNA records everything that we do in our current lifetime and 75 per cent of our DNA holds our memories of our previous lives.

If we go to someone who can read past lives, they are psychically communicating with your higher self who is informing them of the relevant memories contained within your DNA; they are not reading your history from the Akashic as the Akashic does not record personal memories (see also Chapter Two).

In recent years, several people have postulated that the Akashic is formed in ways similar to holograms. The Akashic is not a holographic matrix.

A hologram is formed when an object is targeted by "coherent light", such as the light generated by lasers. The object is illuminated by this light and the reflection of that light is recorded on a photographically prepared glass plate. The image produced by this process is a three dimensional "photograph" of the object. If the glass plate is broken, each and every fragment of glass also contains a full three dimensional image of the original object.

Whilst I can see how it is possible to be misled into thinking that memories can be recorded in the same way as a holographic photograph is made, the reality is that the Akashic is not "fixed" in the way that a photograph is but, whilst not being able to be changed, it is interactive. In other words, it is possible to "enter" into the events the Akashic records but only as an observer.

A hologram can be likened to the type of snap-shot we take with a stills camera. The records contained within the Akashic, in comparison, are more along the lines of the moving snap-shot images envisaged by JK Rowling in her Harry Potter books and films.

As we undergo our current shift in consciousness, we begin to remember who we are and our place within the Universal whole. Unfortunately, we have all been conditioned by religions and by historians who tell our history in an incomplete and biased way and so, as our memories return, what we need is a clear record of our true histories into which our emerging memories can be placed. The Akashic is just a record of events as they occurred and recorded in such a way that is without bias or any pre-conceptions.

So this is what this book is about; a history of our Universe but with particular emphasis on our solar system and the role the souls who have become known as humans have played within that history. Hopefully, by the time this book is finished, we will be able to place into its correct context the change we are currently undergoing.

Chapter One

The Present

Well, we seem to have arrived somewhere new, we are just not sure where. All of the predictions in the Mayan Prophesies, the Hopi Prophesies as well as many other ancient predictions all seem to be fitting in with the final "rounds" of the Mayan Calendar which terminates on the 21st December 2012.

But what does all this mean?

Essentially, we have arrived at the end of a process, a plan, which was designed to allow us to return to our natural state of being a complete "Human Being".

A Human Being is defined as a physical humanoid who has a body which is able to accommodate the whole of the soul. For the past 7,000 years we have not been able to meet this definition and so have been, effectively, "sub-human". By that I mean that we might have a humanoid physical body but our bodies have only been able to hold about one quarter of our total soul.

This sub-human state has meant that we have largely forgotten who and what we are and what our purpose on Earth actually is. As we undergo a radical change in our fundamental energy patterns, we are beginning to wake up to the potential that is intrinsic to all of us.

The 21st of December 2012 is not, as many have interpreted it, the "end of the world" but is the end of a cycle. To put this into perspective, here is an ancient Chinese proverb:

"What the caterpillar calls the end of life, the master calls a butterfly"
(Chuang Tse – Chinese philosopher died 275 BC).

This proverb perfectly sums up where we currently are. For seven thousand years our level of being is related to being the caterpillar. Our current state (1996 – 2011) is that we are "pupating" and by the end of December 2012, at the latest, we will have emerged into the butterfly.

In order to achieve this state of "emergence" we have had to change the fundamental energy patterns of ourselves and the planet. The reasons for this energy change are explored throughout the rest of this book, but the level of change is quite considerable and it is worth looking at the magnitude of this change here.

If you look at Illustration One, what is represented there is the way in which the energy frequencies connected with us and the Earth have changed in recent years.

In order for us to be physical on this planet, the Earth has always produced a "base-note" frequency of 7.56 Hz (that is a frequency of 7.56 cycles per second). Don't worry if you do not understand cycles per second or Hz, it is the value of the level of change that is important.

The Earth's own frequency is that which allows the soul to take on physical form and also, through our "root" chakra, connects us to the Earth.

This "base-note" frequency has been in place ever since the Earth was formed. Every living thing that exists on Earth resonated at this energy frequency. However, many thousands of years ago we realised that this frequency was too low to allow us to maintain the whole of the soul within the body but we did not know to what level the frequency should be raised in order to allow us to fulfil our full potential.

The search to find the required frequency is what The Human Plan has been all about. We have spent 7,000 years living a series of lifetimes (reincarnation) gaining knowledge of how to be fully in tune with the Earth in order for us to bring the whole of the soul back into the body.

This whole learning process has worked both ways. As we have gained knowledge, so has the Earth – all of this accumulated knowledge being stored within the Akashic – once we, jointly and collectively, felt that we knew what the answer was, the Earth took action.

In May 2000, the Earth raised Her base-note frequency to 3.5 kHz (3 thousand five hundred cycles per second) as this was the new energy frequency that was felt to be correct (see Illustration One).

Unfortunately, humans being humans, we were a little slow in responding in the same way and it has taken us a further 10 years to arrive at the point where we can accelerate our own energies.

This is what happened at the start of November 2010. As can be seen in Illustration One, we had raised our own frequencies a little (to around 13 Hz) but then the graph begins to curve and then rise. By the start of November 2011 we will have caught up with the changes the Earth has already made and be in a position to resonate at 3.5 kHz allowing us to reintegrate the whole of the soul back into the body and, for the first time in 7,000 years, once again become true Human Beings.

By the time we reach the end of November 2011, we will once again be resonating fully with the frequencies of the Earth. Once we have achieved that, we can finally draw the rest of the soul in to the body which we will need to achieve before the 21st of December 2012.

In order to achieve this new state of being, we all have a choice – do we fulfil our promise or do we not? Nobody is standing in judgement of us – except ourselves. Only we can decide if we undergo this process of change, nobody can decide for us.

Ascension

In recent years, there has been a huge amount of information produced which suggests that in order to make this level of change, we need to "Ascend" to a "5th Dimension" and that the only way that this "Ascension" can be achieved is to leave the Earth transported by "friendly Aliens" who are part of "Ashtar Command".

Let us think about that for a second. We (humans) have spent 7,000 years living a series of challenging lifetimes working with the Earth to find out what is necessary for humans to exist on Earth. Just at the point where we collectively work out the answer, we are meant to be transported OFF the planet by Aliens. Can you actually see any sense in that? No, and neither can I.

Even the concept of a "5th" dimension is bizarre as to talk in those terms is to fundamentally misunderstand the make-up of the Earth, the solar system and the energy structures of the Universe (see Chapter Two).

The term "dimension" has two meanings:

Firstly, there are physical dimensions – a means by which we can locate ourselves in the space we occupy. These are the physical dimensions that give us our "three-dimensional" world. In this sense, dimensions are length, depth and height. Scientists have been attempting to add a fourth dimension of time but this attempt has largely proved unsuccessful.

Secondly, a dimension can be seen as being a collection of energy frequencies which encompass all of the frequencies that come before the dimensional marker. In this sense, our solar system already contains hundreds of dimensions and the dimensions contained within our Universe run to many, many billions.

So "Ascending to a 5th dimension" is a meaningless concept. The expression does not fit in with our three dimensional world nor does it fit within our multi-dimensional solar system.

This whole thing with Ashtar Command turns out to be a deliberate attempt to mislead us and misdirect us from our chosen paths and, fortunately, many who originally fell for this subterfuge are now waking up to reality and pulling themselves back to where they really need to be.

However, freedom of choice means just that; the absolute freedom to choose the direction of our lives. Whilst many millions of people have chosen to take part in this change, an even greater number have not. For those who have chosen not to fulfil their human potential, they will be leaving their bodies behind, at some point in the near future, and returning to their place of soul origin (see Chapter Three). Just when these people will die is still open to conjecture. However, this process of leaving the Earth is well under way.

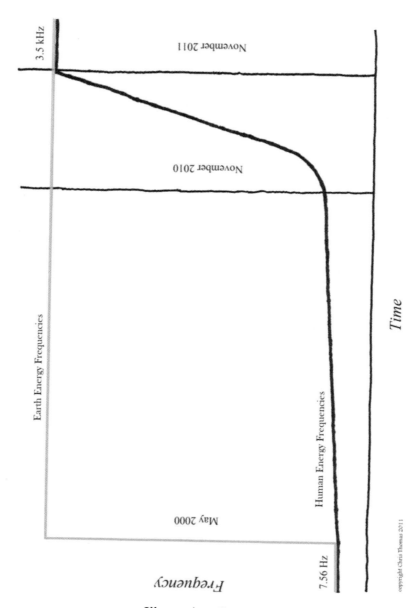

Illustration One
Energy Frequency Change

The beginning of this process of final change began in 1996 when a huge new energy source was connected to the Earth. This clean new energy fired up our plans for change and the first wave of the decision to stay or to leave was made then. Since that initial decision, many millions of people have acted on their choice and have died. In tandem with this decision to leave is the choice of whether to be born. For many souls, the decision to be born into a new body has been delayed until we have completed our process of change.

In light of these choices, we currently have the lowest birth rate ever recorded in human history and the highest death rate – both figures being representational of the proportion to people living. In other words, the global, human population has been rapidly diminishing since 1996.

I appreciate that this view is greatly at odds with the "official" figures given out by governments but, if you closely examine government figures of each country you will find that the population numbers of western countries are either stabilised or are growing because of immigration. In non-western countries, the population figures are dropping markedly. Countries like Rumania, for example, have populations that have dropped by up to 90 per cent in recent years. In overall terms, the global population is now almost one half of what it was in 1996.

To explain what all of this is leading to and what the future holds for us, we will leave until later (see Chapter Fourteen). But to understand where we have come from and how we fit into the universal whole we need to start at the beginning...

Chapter Two

In The Beginning . . .

In the beginning was the thought and the thought was with God.

This is how the first line of the book of Genesis in The Old Testament should read. It is usually expressed as "In the beginning was the word and the word was with God" however, a Hebrew scholar I used to know, David Hadda, returned to the oldest texts he could find and found that "word" had been mistranslated and should, instead, be read as "thought".

The revised text is much closer to the reality of the situation than the original text as our Universe, indeed all of Creation, began with a thought and the Thought was: "what would happen if..."

In the case of our Universe, the Thought was "what would happen if there were free-moving and free-acting beings who were totally free to choose their thoughts and actions". Around about fourteen Billion years ago, we began to explore the Creator's thought.

But, who is this "Creator"?

Everybody has some kind of mental image of "God" ranging from the agnostic non-existent through the naïve burly six foot man with long flowing silver hair and bushy white beard to an image that comes close to the reality.

I use the word "Creator" as opposed to the word "God" because it avoids all of the various interpretations and religious images which could be confusing, The Akashic's memory of our Creator is of a consciousness, a vast eternal being that encompasses everything that is and everything that could be (see Illustration Two).

The image given in Illustration Two is the closest I can manage given the limitations of trying to portray a consciousness with the physical tools I have available to me. The image is obviously not exact but it does give some idea of the reality of the scale of the Creator's form.

The Creator exists in a void where, essentially, nothing else exists. So this is a free-floating Being, a Being not connected to anything or anywhere, It just exists. The time of It's existence is immeasurable, and certainly unknown within the Akashic. This being is neither male nor female and, strictly speaking, not even an "it", the Creator just is what It is. It could, of course, be the case that many such "Creators" exist within this void but there is no way of finding out this information, certainly not from the perspective of Earth.

Our Creator is a thinking being, It wishes to explore, to "know" and in Its exploration of these thoughts, It builds a structure of energy around It's thoughts. It is in this way that universes come into being.

The illustration shows the Creator in the centre with Universes clustered around. The illustration only shows four universes out of the present eleven. There will eventually be thirteen all together, each exploring their own "Thought" and each generating their own version of the Akashic.

The Act of Creation

A Universe is born with a Thought, a kind of "what would happen if...". Once the Thought has occurred, an energy envelope develops into which all of the energy patterns and combinations of energy are installed which allow that particular Thought to be explored. In order to explore all of the possibilities that could present themselves, this universal envelope is filled with the energy patterns that coincide with the Thought itself. Once the structure of the universe is established, the next act is to Create free-moving and free-acting "souls" who will explore the full extent of the Thought on the Creator's behalf.

Illustration Two
A Representation of the "Creator"
25

There are currently eleven universes in existence, each exploring different Thoughts and each being of different ages and in different stages of exploration.

In our Universe, the Thought we are exploring is that of freedom of choice. In other words, every soul that exists within this Universe has the absolute right to choose its own actions and was the very first universe to be built. The only limiting factor to this universal right is that no soul can act in such a way as to remove the right, or the ability of others, to exercise their own freedom of choice.

Fourteen billion, three hundred and twenty six million, two hundred and seventy nine thousand, three hundred and ninety two years ago, our Universe was constructed (14,376,279,393) - as of 2011.

Once the Universal envelope was completed, the first Created beings were introduced. These first beings are thirteen in number and, effectively, make up the Universal envelope itself. These beings do not have any physical form or density but are pure soul energy. These "Thirteen" are charged with the task of maintaining the balance of energies within our Universe and, in fulfilling this role, also act as co-creators.

These Thirteen are immense beings who, collectively, encompass all of the many millions of dimensions of energy that comprise our Universe and can, therefore, be thought of as comprising the Universal envelope itself especially as they are not free-moving.

The first act of the Thirteen was to construct the Akashic. The Akashic is an energy field that fills the Universal void. As an event occurs, the field warps and forms into vortices that carry the energy of the memory that it records. Once these vortices are formed, they cannot be altered; the memory they record is recorded for all time.

This is why the Akashic is such a reliable source of information; it only records events as they occur and records without bias or interpretation and cannot be manipulated into recording something false nor can the recorded memories be altered to reflect someone's agenda.

The purpose of the Akashic is to keep the Creator informed of what is occurring within a particular universe. In this way, the Creator monitors events but does not control events.

In our Universe, in particular, where every soul has absolute freedom of choice to choose their actions, why would the Creator interfere or direct an individual's actions? To do so would totally negate the concept of "freedom of choice". There is no point in imbuing a soul with the freedom to choose and then taking that ability to choose away from them.

It is also in this way that the Creator is not a vengeful "God". The Creator does not punish, to punish someone implies that a wrongful action has been taken. If all is freedom of choice then all choices exist and no action can be wrong. These concepts of "God" are man-made and arose at a time early in human history; they are not Universal concepts (see Chapter Thirteen).

Once the universal envelope was in place and the Thirteen monitoring events, the next act of Creation occurred. This was the Creation of souls who would be able to support and nurture other souls. By this I mean those souls we call galaxies.

In appearance, galaxies reflect the true form of the Creator (see Illustration Number Two) and are souls who have chosen to exist in such a way as to allow other, smaller, souls to carry out their own choices.

A galaxy is an energy "swirl" which contains the energy potential to give other souls form – by this I mean the souls who make up solar systems or individual planets.

As humans, we are used to thinking of everything as being solid objects. The Earth we stand on, the solar system we inhabit and the galaxy we are a part of we have been led to believe are made of solid matter, but they are not. Each galaxy and solar system is first and foremost a soul and it is the energies of which that individual soul is comprised that determine its makeup – see later.

The energies that these souls are comprised of we know as electro-magnetic energies. The Universe is not held together by gravity but by electro-magnetism. Another word for electro-magnetism is soul and another word for soul is consciousness. In this way, our Universe, all of the galaxies, all of the solar systems and many individual planets are consciousnesses – we live in a conscious Universe.

Universal Development

Once the galaxies, solar systems and planets were in place, the next phase of development could begin.

Whilst galaxies, solar systems and individual planets are exercising their free choice, their free actions are limited and, therefore, in order to explore the Creator's thought, free-moving and free-acting souls were required.

In order to explore the potential and possibilities offered by our Universe, souls were specially Created that are, essentially, human in form. This does not mean that "we were made in God's image" (see Illustration Number Two and Chapter Three) but that this form was considered to be the most efficient to carry out the task we were charged with.

One hundred million years ago, the first of these free-acting, free-moving, humanoid souls were Created.

The Six Non-Physical Races

There are six of these first-Created races, each comprising many billions of souls. Each of these races inhabited their own planet located in very different regions of the Universe.

These souls do not have any "physical" density, they exist in a form that is pure soul energy but roughly human in shape. These "first-born" souls are what most people would consider to be "Angels", when interpreted from the romanticised Victorian viewpoint. When interpreted from a Biblical viewpoint, the term "Angel" actually means something entirely different – it just means "Messenger".

These six "non-physical" races are very similar in characteristics, so similar, in fact, that we humans would not be able to tell any differences between them. Once these non-physical beings settled onto their respective regions of space, they began to explore their surroundings.

These beings only communicate psychically, both in "face to face" encounters or across their home planets and so do not require any form of communication technology. In this way, they exist in total silence.

They do not require any form of food as they sustain themselves by drawing into themselves the energy patterns that exist around them – to us, it would look as though they live on fresh air.

They do share their worlds with other forms of life; plants and animals, with which they also communicate psychically. Animal and plant forms are the creation of the planet on which they exist; the Creator does not bring these forms to life - they are a creation of the particular planet. The plants and animals that exist on these non-physical planets are also non-physical in nature.

These six races all developed very rapidly and began to explore the regions of space in which they existed. In their explorations, they encountered each other and began to explore the Universe sharing all of their experiences and knowledge with each of the other non-physical races. In this way, although they were originally six independent races they can be seen as one. Certainly, from a human perspective, we would not be able to differentiate between the races but would see all six as being of one race.

However, the six non-physical races have one major limitation. It might not seem that way to us as they can travel freely throughout the whole of the Universe without ships – they just think themselves where they want to go and travel along the thought. This form of travel allows them to journey anywhere through space as they do not need any form of atmosphere or food. But they cannot interact with anything. By that I mean they can "feel" energies, they can observe events but they cannot partake in those events because to take part in events that occur you need to have a physical response and not just an energetic response.

Now, this is where time begins to get a little bit funny – from our perspective in any way.

We perceive time as being a function of the speed at which light travels. In our solar system light travels at 300,000,000 metres per second (186,000 miles per hour). However, light only travels at that speed locally to us. In other parts of the Universe, light travels at vastly different speeds and so time passes at speeds to match. What we perceive as one year of elapsed time will appear to be minutes in one part of the Universe or just seconds in another.

The reason for mentioning time here is to do with how the non-physical races perceive time as they did not fully appreciate their limitations (of being non-physical) for many millions of our years. However, within their time references, their self realisation took place within decades.

This is where the Akashic comes in very useful. As the non-physical races began to understand that they had limited abilities, their understanding was recorded within the Akashic. This information was then picked up by the Thirteen and also the Creator.

There then followed "discussions" between the Creator, the Thirteen and the six non-physical races as to how this limitation could be overcome.

The agreed solution was to Create new races who could physically interact with their environments. By physically interacting, these new more physical races would be more able to explore all of the possibilities our Universe has to offer and through exploration at a more physical level of being, the Creator's original Thought (what would happen if...?) could be better answered.

The "Physical" Races

Two new developments were agreed upon. This agreement was reached by the Creator, the Thirteen and the six non-physical races all exercising their free choice and willingness to explore.

The agreement was this:

The first part: - seven new races would be Created who had a physical nature and a physical form. They would be Created souls whose physical bodies were part of their soul's structure. In other words, body and soul would be one. These holistic beings would have a natural life-span that ran into many millions of Earth years with their bodies capable of self repair and reconstruction.

The second part of the agreement was that a region of space would be developed where life would exist at physical densities greater than those of the seven new races. The idea behind this was to explore the possibilities offered by being fully physical. The beings who would inhabit this region of space would develop in such a way that members of the six non-physical races could visit and experience physical life for themselves by adopting a physical body to cloak the soul.

In other words, the forms of life that would inhabit this region of space would not have permanent body/soul structures like the seven new races but would have the ability for the soul to leave the body if that was the soul's choice. The soul could also return, at a later date, and build for itself a new body. This form of life was decided upon so that the non-physical races could leave this region of space and return to their soul origins if they did not like what these new planets had to offer.

These decisions are an example of how the Akashic was designed to work. The Akashic records events and provides "feedback" to the Creator so that modifications or adjustments can be made to suit the choices made by those who inhabit our Universe.

By realising their limitations, the six non-physical races were able to communicate directly with the Creator and make new choices of how best to explore the possibilities offered by our Universe.

New Developments

With the decisions made, these new developments were put into action, both at the same time.

To help differentiate between these new races, the Akashic records that the seven new races are designated as "semi-physical" whilst the physical race is known as "Human".

Both of these developments were begun 50 million years ago – these are years in terms of how we measure them on Earth.

A "request" was put out to the Universe for regions of space who would "volunteer" to be the host for these new races.

For the semi-physical races, seven very different regions chose to be a part of this new development. Each of these regions encompasses a number of different galaxies. Whilst each galaxy is an individual soul, several agreed to work together to provide the maximum potential for development and exploration.

Within one of these "galactic collectives", one solar system chose to be the "home world" for where one of the new semi-physical races could begin their new existence.

As the "human" aspect of these new developments was to be an "experiment" in physical life, it was felt that only a single solar system was required, initially, to explore the possibilities on offer.

One galaxy chose to be the host and a new solar system was brought into being to be the "home worlds" for "Human" life.

To explain how these developments were enacted, we will start with the story of the development of the seven semi-physical races.

Chapter Three

The Semi-Physical Races

In order to bring about sentient life, a particular process has to be undergone.

The first thing that needs to happen is that a Creationery thought must occur. Once the thought is in place, a template must be made of what form this new life-form will take. This template is made of energy which contains all of the necessary organs and limbs that this new form of life will require.

With the formation of the seven new regions that were to be the "home planets" for the semi-physical races, the only template that had been tried in this Universe was the form that the non-physical races took. It was this "humanoid" template that was adopted by these new planets.

The creation of life, throughout this whole Universe, follows the same patterns. The "home planet" designs the templates for the forms of life that the planet considers to be the most suitable for the conditions that prevail. The energy template is then given form from the substance of the planet itself. This process allows for the free choices and free expression of that planet to find expression.

As far as animal and plant life is concerned, these forms of life are purely the creation of the planet concerned. The planet builds the template, gives the template "solid" form and then imbues that solid form – the prototype made from the template – with an aspect of its own consciousness.

However, with "higher" forms of life, the home planet either constructs or adopts the template, the planet then gives the template form from the "matter" from which the planet is constructed but the "soul" of the "higher life" is Created by the Creator.

This is what happened with the birth of the seven semi-physical races; the planet adopted the template shape of the non-physical races, made that template "solid" by utilising the "soil" of the planet but it was the Creator who gave the template life – Created the soul. As the souls were specifically Created for these seven regions, these home planets can be considered their place of "soul origin".

This process of co-creation can take a long time as "prototypes" need to be developed. The basic template giving general outline had been in existence since about 100 million years ago but the semi-physical races had to be viable on planets that were considerably more "physical" than the conditions that existed on the home worlds of the non-physical races.

Many attempts at creating an ideal form had been made whilst working out the best combination of options. These options included: how many limbs worked best? What internal organs were needed? What was to be the function of each of these organs? What was the best location for each organ in relation to its function? As well as a huge number of answers that needed to be found. This was new life in the making and they had to be right.

All in all, finding the answers to all of these questions and eliminating unviable options took a long time and it was around about 30 million years ago that everything was ready and the final act of Creating the souls took place. Once the act of soul creation was finished, it then required that the answers needed to be found to a whole new set of questions.

This exploration of the self, their environment and the galaxies they lived within was something at which the semi-physical races excelled. All of the semi-physical races have immense curiosity along with a want to explore.

In order to explore worlds beyond their home planet, they needed to develop ships. Whilst the non-physical races can travel to anywhere and any when without the need for craft of any kind, the semi-physical races needed to develop transport to protect their more physical bodies.

Each of the seven races developed their own form of technology and they all seem to have arrived at roughly similar solutions. Essentially, the technology developed by these races is non-destructive to their environments – they work with what they have and mould it to their needs without harm or damage. If we contrast these types of technology to the ones we have developed on Earth, you will see what I mean.

For our example, let us look at how forms of transport differ.

On Earth, we have automobiles, trains, planes and rockets. Whilst they have different functions, they all share common factors. They all have bodies made of metal, engines made of metal and fuel made from oil.

To manufacture the metal bodies, metal ore is blasted by explosives or ripped from the earth. Once the ore has been extracted, it is then crushed and a great deal of fuel expended to extract the metal from the ore. What is not metal is then piled up in waste heaps, most of which are very toxic to their environment.

Once the metal is extracted from the ore, it then undergoes further heating and melting which is then moulded into the shapes required – all processes which require vast amounts of energy which is mainly supplied by derivatives of oil.

Once the bodies and engines have been formed, the vehicle then requires a means of propulsion; this is usually in the form of oil which has been refined from its original state.

Oil is found at great distances under the surface. To extract the oil, again, huge amounts of energy are required. The extraction process also generates a huge amount of toxic environmental damage. Once extracted from the ground, the oil then has to be refined by chemical means, again adding toxic waste. When burned in the engines, further environmental damage is created through the engine's exhaust.

This is what I mean by destructive technology.

The semi-physical races are quite different.

To build their ships, they use materials that are readily available within their environment, such as forms of plants.

To build the bodies of their ships, they gather together a collection of the most suitable plants which they then encourage to grow over an energy template built psychically. The plants readily grow over the templates and a ship's hull is easily formed. Once formed in this way, the leaves of the plant are cut and the "leaves" of the plant form an impenetrable hull – something along the lines of what we would describe as an "organic" metal. The plants are not killed or harmed by this process and they can be transplanted for re-use to build other ships. The engines are built in very similar ways.

The power source, used to drive the engines, is also from a natural source.

We saw in Chapter Two that the Universe is electro-magnetic in composition. This electro-magnetic energy is freely available to anyone who wants to use it and it is this energy source that these races use to power their craft.

Everything done within this process of building ships is totally non-destructive and non-harmful either to the environment or to the beings who use these craft.

I know many of you will say that we, on Earth, do not have the psychic potential to do most of the construction work in the same way as these races do and that is true. However, we do have access to the same energy source. Those of you who are familiar with the work of Nikola Tesla will understand what I mean although Tesla called it "Aetheric" energy as opposed to electro-magnetic energy.

Tesla developed a large number of electrical type machines around the turn of the 1900's. One of his major successes was to tap into what he called the "Aether" to provide "free" energy. Essentially, Tesla found a way of powering his car, plane and domestic appliances using electro-magnetic energies. He went as far as to build a major "power station" in America to prove that every electrical-type appliance could be powered in this way. His major financial backers removed their finance when they found out that there was not a profit to be made as, after the initial construction costs, all of the energy to power cars, home appliances etc was free.

Think of it, we could have had cost-free and pollution-free energy for over 100 years but because the oil companies could not make a profit on the energy, Tesla's work was stopped and made secret as has the work of several people who have managed to emulate Tesla's work.

You could argue that we are beginning to change our destructive ways by slowly switching to "Bio-fuels" except that the growing of these crops on prime agricultural land has led to world food prices rising by over 35 per cent. This price increase has led to many thousands of people starving to death and the irony is that the exhaust gasses from burning bio-fuels are more environmentally toxic than burning petrol or oil.

So we continue to be destructive to our environment all for the sake of the greed of a few people.

A Description of the Seven Races

As we saw above, all of the higher forms of life are an act of co-creation; the body is formed by the consciousness of the home planet but the soul is only created by the Creator. This act of co-creation provides for as large a diversity of life as possible and this is certainly true for the seven semi-physical races created in this way.

Whilst all of these races have a body form that is humanoid in shape, each race is unique in its characteristics and appearance.

What is meant by "semi-physical" is that they have a physical form and a physical density and to each other, they appear as physically solid as we do on Earth. However, if we had a representative of one of these races standing in front of us now, the chances are that we humans would not be able to see them or even sense their presence. This is because these races are constructed of energy frequencies that are far outside of the energy patterns we are used to here on Earth. As our senses have developed to work within our physical environment, we do not have sufficient sensory awareness to "see" the energy frequencies that these races exist at.

I am not going to spend a great deal of time describing these semi-physical races and their home worlds as I have already covered the topic in several of my previous books. So, for now, I will only give a brief description of each and how each has interacted with Earth. The list of these semi-physical races is given in no particular order.

The Pleiadeans

These are a race that originate on the star system we know as the Pleiades. We call it by this name as it is the name these beings gave it.

The Pleiadeans are closest to humans in shape and appearance. They look like one of our Scandinavian races as they are tall and slender with blond hair and blue eyes. (Please note: these are not the "Tall White Nordics" of Area 51 fame – see later for an explanation). They average about 2.4 m (8 ft) in height. They do have male and female forms but do not reproduce – there are no Pleiadean children.

As a race, they have spread out over a number of galaxies, settling on many planets that were compatible with their needs. Those who originate on two of these planets have caused confusion to human UFO watchers as they call themselves Plejaran or Ummite.

The Akashic records the names of all of the worlds that the seven semi-physical races inhabit, some would be familiar to us, the majority would not. In order to avoid the great deal of confusion that has arisen over race names, I have chosen to use their "soul origin" name only. By soul origin I mean the race name that these races have given to themselves which is usually reflected in the name of the planet on which the race first originated.

The Pleiadeans can be described as the Universe's diplomatic corps as they generally become involved in most of the events that take place within our Universe.

They have a long association with Earth but do not make their presence known as they can see that visitors from an "Alien" race would cause too much disruption to human life which would distract us from our chosen aim of soul reintegration. Once we have completed our chosen task, they will no doubt visit us often.

The Sirians

For the same reason as the Pleiadeans, we call this race Sirian as they originate from the star system Sirius.

The Sirians tend to be 1.7m to 1.9m (5ft 8ins to 6ft) tall. They are grey skinned with very slim bodies, arms and legs. Their eyes are all black and quite large with their other facial features not very well defined.

They are master technologists. If a "tool" of any kind is required, the Sirians are usually capable of designing and building them.

The Sirians are very friendly and have no other agenda other than to be helpful.

They have had a long association with the Earth as is reflected in the tribal history of the Dugon tribe of north east Africa. The peoples of the Dugon tribe have traditions that state that they originated on the planets that orbit the stars Sirius "A" and Sirius "B". The accuracy of this tribal knowledge pre-dates, by many hundreds of years, the more recent discoveries by human astronomers and cosmologists.

The NGC 584

This is not the name that these beings call themselves, that name is totally unpronounceable by the human voice box and we do not have sufficient characters in our alphabet to even write their name.

The name "NGC 584" is the astronomer's catalogue number for their home galaxy which is located behind the arc of the Pleiadean star system but is many galaxies distant.

In appearance, they are similar to a human two year old child in that they are about 90cm (2ft 6ins) tall with a head that is proportionately larger than their bodies. They have a red/brown skin colour which is leathery in texture.

The NGC 584 are master geneticists and hold the record of every living thing that has ever existed within this Universe. The worlds on which they live are all "ice planets" and have temperatures that can drop to minus 200 degrees centigrade which is perfect for storing genetic material.

Unlike human geneticists, they do not have any agenda; they just give of their expertise freely and without charge. They have been involved with the Earth for many millions of years and are capable of rebuilding any of the forms of life that human activities have made extinct.

The Greys

These are the classic "Aliens", the short, grey beings with almond shaped black eyes. They do not actually have black eyes; their eyes are yellow with vertical irises. Their home planet has a low level of natural light and so when they leave their home world, they require shading and protection for their eyes.

The Greys are about 1m to 1.1m (3ft to 3ft 6 ins) tall with smooth bodies and not very pronounced facial features.

In temperament, they are a little like human teenagers: emerging into a state of knowledge but unsure about how to deal with it. Their home galaxy is too distant for us to see from Earth and so it does not even have an astronomer's catalogue number. Their name for themselves is also unpronounceable.

Their first real contact with Earth was with the Roswell crash in 1948 and they have been working with the military ever since. The military have mainly been interested in Grey technology which the military mainly use for psychic attack purposes.

The Greys are very interested in human physiology and are responsible for *some* human and animal abductions.

Please note: the vast majority of human and animal abductions and mutilations have been carried out by the military. There seem to be a couple of reasons for this. One is to do with testing of the spread of man-made biological agents and the other is to do with the creation of fear and disinformation.

Speaking of disinformation, there are a number of stories, purported to be by abductees of "teachers" travelling with the Greys; these teachers looking very similar to a praying mantis. Since first hearing these stories, I have searched the Akashic for confirmation of non-terrestrial creatures in the form of a praying mantis and I cannot find any. This leads me to conclude that the existence of these "teachers" is yet another layer of disinformation.

The Blues

Again, their home star system is too distant for astronomers to have catalogued, but it is located behind the constellation of Capricorn and forty galaxies distant.

They are called the Blues as they are covered in short, dark blue hair. They are about 1m (3ft) tall with very short legs and round, barrel-like bodies.

Like the NGC, they have an interest in genetics but are not as knowledgeable as the NGC. In the past, the Blues have worked together with some healers on Earth although that contact has reduced in recent years.

The Blues and Greys frequently travel together.

The Velon

The Velon originate on a star system they call Velus which is located behind the constellation of Sagittarius but twenty three galaxies distant. They are divided into six sub-races which they name: Jjundaa, Oa, Mila, Johnaan, Annunaki and Hathor. They vary in height between 2.4m to 4.5m (8ft to 14ft) and are very similar in appearance to humans.

They live in a solar system with two suns and eight planets; three orbit around one sun and four orbit around the other. The eighth planet, called Nibiru, orbits around both suns.

Some of the names of their sub-races will be familiar as there is a huge volume of channelled material originated by this race.

The Velon are responsible for a vast number of problems on Earth (*see Project Human Extinction - The Ultimate Conspiracy* and *The Annunaki Plan? or The Human Plan?*), so much so that they have acted in ways which remove freedom of choice. The removal of freedom of choice is a "crime" which has warranted a demand for the removal of the Velon from our Universe – this demand being made by every single soul that inhabits this Universe which has also been echoed by the Creator. Most of the many billions of souls who comprise the Velon race complied peacefully with this demand and have left to live in a new solar system that is outside of our universal envelope.

However, 3.5 million Velon have refused to leave and have continued to create and perpetuate problems for us here on Earth (see Chapter Eleven). Fortunately, the energy patterns detailed in Illustration One have modulations which will make it impossible for the remaining Velon to stay in our galaxy.

Crystalline

Now we come to something entirely different. The other six semi-physical races are free moving and free acting individuals, this race is not.

As their name suggests, they are crystalline in form and exist in two different versions. The first are individual crystals which exist in physical isolation on their home planet's surface. These individual crystals vary in height by anything up to 16m (50ft) tall. The second exist in communities of anything up to 1,000 individuals. These communities look a little like crystal glaciers.

Their home world is on the other side of the universe from us and so fall far out of the range of our telescopes to "see" them.

Although they are literally rooted to their planet, it does not mean that they cannot travel. This they do by a method we would call "remote viewing". In other words they can project their consciousness far beyond their home galaxies and travel, at will, throughout virtually the whole Universe.

So these are the seven semi-physical races. As you can see, they have a great deal of variety in form although none of them can be described as "reptilian" which some people will find surprising. However, there was a race of "reptilian" beings that did have a major impact on our Universe and we will describe who and what they are, and their impact, in Chapter Eleven.

All of the races, except for the Crystalline, have spread out from their home worlds and have colonised many other galaxies and planets. Wherever they have settled, their arrival has stimulated the planetary consciousness of their new planet to develop forms of life of their own. These life-forms are along the lines of animals and plants and so many, many millions of planets support life of this nature. So we do not have a Universe devoid of life, as our scientists are fond of telling us, but there is an abundance and variety of life which is startling in its diversity.

Universal Change

There is, however, always room for change and new choices to be made. In this respect, several of the semi-physical races are beginning to undergo their own change and development.

The semi-physical races are beings whose form was specifically designed to be a soul and body combination which is very difficult to change. In our, human, existence, we are a soul that builds for itself a body; when the soul has gained enough experience from a particular human lifetime, the soul removes itself from the body and moves on to other experiences and other lives. For the semi-physical races, their soul/body combination is, in many ways, eternal and so they see the abilities and adaptability of the non-physical races as being a step forwards in evolution and so this is the change which some of the semi-physical races are attempting to undergo – to leave their bodies behind and become pure soul energy.

A number of individuals were at the forefront of this progression and found a way of achieving this pure energy state. Most of those who successfully achieved the ability to leave their bodies behind moved to Earth and took on human form – see Chapter Seven.

Conversely, a number of individuals from the non-physical races have decided that they have experienced all that they wish to experience in this Universe and are leaving to re-merge their souls with the Creator.

Whilst we humans undergo our own changes of levels of consciousness, so are others throughout this Universe and it is the work we have carried out on Earth that is making this level of change possible.

Chapter Four

Our Solar System

Much of what is to follow here is totally at odds with scientific thinking. The solar system, the Earth, human development and the development of plants and animals bears very little resemblance to the history we are taught in schools. The biggest surprise of all is the time frames involved.

Scientists will tell you that the Earth is 4,000,000,000 (4 billion) years old. The way in which they arrived at this figure is, to put it mildly, strange. The age is not based on rocks or fossils that are of this Earth but from a meteorite. This meteorite has an unknown origin; it could have arrived here from anywhere throughout our galaxy. I am not sure what dating technique they used to put an age to this alien rock but, whatever it is, it is wrong by a factor of one hundred.

Our Universe underwent a huge phase of development 60 million years ago (see Chapter Two) which included laying the foundations for both the semi-physical races and our solar system.

We discussed the semi-physical races in Chapter Three so as we move on to look at the development of our solar system, the key date is 60 million years ago.

Our solar system is an experiment, an experiment in new forms of life that exist nowhere else throughout the whole of Creation. The experiment is to find out if life can be successful at the combination of energy patterns we know as "physical". Remember that: everything is comprised of energy, nothing is "solid", it is only the way in which our brains perceive these combinations of energy that make us believe that we, and the world around us, is physical.

When the request went out for a galaxy to host this new experiment, of those that responded a galaxy was chosen that was well away from the main-stream activities of the Universe. A quiet backwater that would not be too heavily influenced by what else went on in the Universe but also the activities that took place here would not, conversely, affect the rest of the Universe in return.

Once the "host" galaxy was chosen, an area was set aside so that a new solar system could be constructed. This was, again, on the boundaries of our home galaxy so that nothing affected what happened here.

The Development of Our Solar System

The first step in the development of our solar system was to construct an energy "envelope" which combined together all of the energy patterns and number of energy dimensions necessary for life to develop at the energy combinations compatible with physical life. This envelope originally contained 285 dimensions, as we began to re-awaken in 1996, this figure increased to 396 dimensions (a dimension, in this sense, is a collection of energy frequencies and the dimensional marker takes note of the change between one set of frequencies and the next highest collection of frequencies – a little like the markers on a radio scale).

This energy envelope has two "gateways" that allow for the free access of the other races. One gateway coincides with the central belt on the constellation of Orion and connects in to the rest of the Universe. The other coincides with the constellation of Draco and connects to the realms of the semi-physical races – see Illustration Three.

Once this envelope was complete, the consciousnesses (souls) who were to build the planets within the solar system then arrived and set to work building their respective planets.

This is something else which makes our solar system unique. In other galaxies, solar systems are constructed by a single consciousness, this consciousness usually being the primary sun of that solar system. With our solar system, because it was to be such a new experiment, it was decided that each of the planets, and the sun, would be separate consciousnesses to allow for the maximum opportunity for expression and originality.

The solar system originally contained thirteen planets plus the sun. You may have noticed by now that the number thirteen figures a great deal in Creation. There will eventually be thirteen universes, there are the Thirteen beings who maintain the balance of energies within this Universe and there are thirteen races – six non-physical and seven semi-physical. Thirteen is the whole number of the Creator.

With the 13 planetary consciousnesses in place, they began to build for themselves the structure of their planets and forty million years ago, the solar system was ready to begin experimenting with life.
This is the true age of the oldest of the solar system's rocks – forty million years old.

As mentioned in Chapter Two, Universal life develops in one of two ways; there is an act of "primary" Creation which brings about galaxies, solar systems and free-moving and free-acting souls and then there is the creation of life that inhabits solar systems.
Where the planets of a solar system are an aspect of that solar systems primary consciousness, usually its sun, then all other forms of life, such as plants and animals, are created by that solar system consciousness.
With our solar system, the process of creating plant and animal life was carried out by the individual planets.
As our solar system is an experiment, it was decided that there should be as large a diversity of life as possible. In this way, it meant that if no suitable life-forms were developed by one planet, there would be 12 others to choose from.

However, the choice to use "physical" energies to bring about life proved to be immensely productive and every single planet within our solar system developed life. In other words, all thirteen planets created and developed life, all of them in forms which reflected the planetary consciousness's concept of what physical life should be like.
Every one of the original thirteen planets within our solar system developed an atmosphere and plants and animals and then went on to experiment with a "higher" life-form that was usually humanoid in

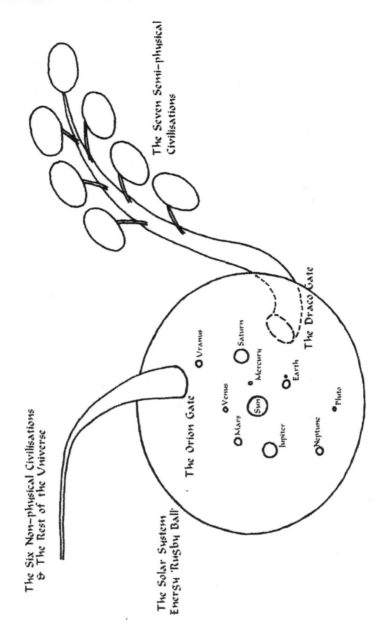

Illustration Number Three
Our Solar System & Its Gateways

shape and was capable of being a "home" for one of the souls who are of the six non-physical races.

Just to emphasise this: every planet within our solar system once supported life.

It is difficult to accept this now as, apart from Earth, all of the other planets in our solar system appear devoid of life. This is unfortunately true, apart from one planetary moon. But, as we on Earth undergo change, so does the solar system and life is now beginning to re-emerge.

So, how does life develop on a planet? Where do the basic ideas and forms come from and how do we arrive at the forms of life we know today?

The first question is what is to be the basic structure of life-forms to be made from? On Earth we have identified our basic atomic structure to be carbon. But it could easily have been silicone or something quartz-like or even atomic structures that are totally unknown on Earth. All of these options exist throughout the Universe.

But, eventually, the general consensus was that carbon seemed to be the most flexible option.

Next, what kind of atmosphere? The gasses of the atmosphere needed to be compatible with carbon and also to help life grow. Again, throughout the solar system the choice was of a combination of oxygen and carbon dioxide, in varying ratios, together with a mix of other gasses unique to each individual planet.

Water? Should it be fresh water, salt water of some kind or a combination of the two? Again, each planet chose its own combination.

Once these important factors were decided upon, the next stage was to begin designing plants and animals. By plants I mean everything from the smallest fungus up to the biggest trees and by animals I mean everything from the smallest bacteria up to the biggest Blue Whale.

All life needed to be designed from scratch. Ours was a new solar system where nothing existed before and the solar system was experimenting with energy patterns that did not exist anywhere else within the whole of Creation so there was nothing pre-existing to work with.

To help in this plight, the solar system asked for help, advice and guidance from the NGC 584. As discussed in the last chapter, the NGC are master geneticists. They developed the ability to travel to virtually any region of the Universe and had amassed a huge body of knowledge of the forms of life that exist throughout the whole universe very early on in their own development.

Given the whole solar system was experimental and unique; a strategy for life was developed very early on in each planet's development.

The process of building life is one where an energy "template" is developed. This template has the outline of the finished life and contains the energy equivalent of muscles, internal organs, blood vessels etc for animals or sap channels and structure for plants and trees. Once the template is complete, it becomes part of a mass consciousness that has been built by the planet's consciousness. The template is then given physical form by blending together elements from the soil of the planet. Once one finished plant or animal exists, the mass consciousness of that plant or animal then spreads it out over the planet's surface.

However, one other component is also built into the template and that is an ability to evolve.

A form of life cannot evolve unless it has first been created and there is no point creating a form of life if it cannot evolve in the directions its environment requires. Life begins with a creationery act, in this case the consciousness of the planet concerned, but then evolves to fit its local environment. If the form of life is not capable of evolution then it does not fit its environment, the template becomes weakened and the life form's mass consciousness collapses and disappears and that form of life no longer exists.

However, where a form of life does evolve, we end up with a huge variety of life; life whose only limits are the choices of the home planet.

The way in which the NGC work is this: they work with the planet's consciousness to help develop a particular template. Once the template is completed, the NGC then design the DNA that is required. With the template and the DNA in place, elements from the planet's soil are blended in to the template to give the form of life substance. The planet generates a mass consciousness, a "group" soul, which then imbues that life form with life.

Alternatively, the NGC suggest a form of life that they have encountered on other worlds. If the planet agrees, the NGC bring the template from the originating planet and the process given above begins.

Where large quantities of a particular form of life are required, such as bacteria, the NGC will prepare these in advance and transport the bacteria to the planet using comets.

Comets are a form of consciousness, about the level of say a dog, who build around themselves a body of ice. Whilst the ice is forming, the NGC saturate it with the required bacteria and send the comet to the chosen planet. By seeding large numbers of comets in this way, a large quantity of bacteria can be distributed over the planet's surface at the same time; the comet's ice melting to provide sustenance for the bacteria's immediate needs until they have integrated themselves into the planet. The consciousness that is the comet then returns to its place of origin to start the process again.

The consciousness of the planet is brought into being in an act of primary Creation by the Creator but the life that the planet supports is the creation of the planet itself; the Creator plays no part in bringing about these forms of life.

The forms of life that inhabit a planet are brought about by the choices of the planet and, like all expressions of freedom of choice, the Creator does not interfere. Why would the Creator bring about a universe that is built around the energies of freedom of choice and then not allow the Created souls to exercise their freedom to choose? If the Creator interfered in this way, it would destroy this Universe as the Creator would be acting in a way that removes freedom of choice.

Chapter Five

The Development of Life on Earth

Forty million years ago, the planets of our solar system were fully formed and beginning to explore the potential that physical life had to offer. Or at least twelve of the thirteen planets had begun to explore physical life.

The Earth was a little different. The Earth's consciousness waited and watched. She did not want to leap in to the situation, but thought very deeply about the forms of life She wanted to develop and nurture. Whilst the other planets were trying out every form of life they could think of, the Earth spent Her time making sure that she had the basics right before moving on.

Her first task was to sort out the balance between water and atmosphere and how both could work together to be suitable places where new life would be developing. This she achieved by flooding her surface with water to an extent far greater than any other planet and developing forms of bacteria which could produce various chemical mixes for the air around the planet.

Slowly, She began to develop plant forms that, again, balanced or enriched the air. The next stage was to develop small animals that could fulfil all of their needs by eating and recycling the plants. This first stage of Creating life began only 25 million years ago.

As this new life began to spread and evolve, the planet began to grow in size. Originally, like all of the planets within our solar system, they began their life-creating period at about 50 per cent, one half, of their current diameters. As new life began to flourish, the planet's levels of consciousness began to grow and, with that growth of consciousness, the planet grew as well.

The scientific view is that the Earth has always been the same size as She is now with major migrations of the continents (Continental Drift) taking place every few million years which, for the scientists, explains why some of the continents fit together like pieces of a jigsaw. This same argument is used to explain how the same plant and animal species can live on continents that are currently thousands of miles apart. The same applies to differing sea levels. The scientific belief is that there has been massive freezing of the planet's surface – Ice Ages – occurring from time to time which explains why sea levels have risen and fallen.

The whole scientific theory of tectonic plate movement and regular Ice Ages is immensely complex and even more convoluted in its explanations. Everything becomes extremely simple if the reality recorded within the Akashic is followed; the Earth started off small and then expanded in size. There have also been periods where she contracted again and we will discuss those later.

The Birth of the Faerie

Along with the development of plants, the Earth decided that she needed a new form of life that would look after the plants whilst the Earth began to concentrate on more human prototypes.

Twenty million years ago, the Faerie were Created to fulfil this purpose and, along with the Faerie, came the Sidhé. The Sidhé can be considered as the "management" of the Faerie, those who direct the actions and activities of "the little people" to ensure that the plants are maintained at their peak condition to allow for maximum evolution.

It was also at this time that a member of one of the six non-physical races came to help with the development of plants on Earth and began to work very closely with the Sidhé and the Faerie whilst the planet concentrated on the human prototypes. In Celtic traditions, this soul from the non-physical races is known as "The Lady" and she still lives and works with the Sidhé and the Faerie although she very often takes on human form.

All of the other planets in the solar system also had their equivalent of "The Lady"; a member of the non-physical races who worked with plant life on those planets.

The Development of Human Life

The Earth might have been comparatively slow in starting Her Creationery work but she soon began to catch up with the other planets. All kinds of life were developed and allowed to evolve. If the life-form did not evolve to the Earth's satisfaction, it was removed. Sometimes, She decided to start again with a totally clean "sweep" of the planet's surface by shrinking the planet's size and washing all life away but keeping the templates of the most promising forms of life for when she began again.

Everything was tried; from the miniscule to the giant, but always She had in mind the primary purpose of our solar system – could we develop a form of life that was roughly humanoid in shape and capable of accommodating the whole soul.

At every stage of Her experimentation, She tried a collection of new human types. Some were like reptiles, some like fish or a combination of the two. At any time during these early experiments, there were never less than six possible human forms on the planet.

Eventually, She developed mammals – animals capable of giving birth to live young – on both land and in the seas. This form of life looked very promising as they were adaptable and numerous different versions were developed and many unsuccessful ones discarded.

By about 5 million years ago, there were five human "prototypes" which looked very promising. These ranged from "Gigantopithicus" at around 3m to 3.5m (9ft to 11ft) to the pygmy at about 0.9m (2ft 6ins) with "Neanderthal Man" somewhere in the middle. Most lived on the land but two were amphibious. All of these prototypes lived in various regions and shared the planet with all of the other forms of life, including the dinosaurs, especially when dinosaurs were in the process of "dying out".

Planetary Guardians

With the development of successful human prototypes, the Thirteen beings who maintain the balance of energies of this Universe took a much closer interest in the developments taking place within the solar system. In order to be kept informed of progress, as well as to be a "channel" for any additional energies that might be required, the Thirteen Created "Guardians". Each of the thirteen planets within our solar system had a Guardian created specifically for them.

On Earth, the Guardian was given a name by the Sidhé that reflected the Guardian's role; the name is still used in Celtic traditions and means "the creator of energy" or Merlin. In other traditions, this Guardian is known by other names, for example: Wohana-wish-hay by Native Americans and Zamna in South America.

The role of these Guardians is to ensure that each planet has sufficient energies to fulfil their chosen task; the development of a humanoid life-form capable of accommodating the whole of a soul. They were also created to protect the planet they were appointed to. In this way, Merlin arrived on Earth 4 million years ago.

I am not going to spend much time detailing Merlin's involvement with the Earth or the role "he" has played in human history. If you wish to know a little more about this character, see *"Planet Earth – The Universe's Experiment"*.

The Destruction of the Solar System

Shortly following the arrival of the planetary Guardians, four of the planets within our solar system made a choice that was to have devastating affects on the life we share our solar system with.

Our Universe is exploring the Thought of freedom of choice. Every soul that exists within this Universe has the absolute right to freely choose their own actions. Three million nine hundred thousand (3.9m) years ago, four of the planetary consciousnesses decided to leave our solar system and abandon the work they had carried out in developing physical forms of life.

All of the life-forms that they had developed were either adopted by the remaining planets or were preserved by the NGC. Once the planets were clear of life, the planetary consciousness left their planet with very unexpected consequences.

There are very many millions of solar systems throughout our Universe. In comparison to their home galaxy, solar systems have much shorter life-spans. When the solar system consciousness decides to move on, the consciousness leaves the planet or, more usually, their solar system and the planets and sun slowly disintegrate with the galaxy taking back to itself the energies used to construct the sun and planets over a period of time.

However, our solar system is different and it was not understood just how different it was until the first two planetary consciousnesses left their planets.

Ours is a physical solar system and the planets are made from energies that are massively compressed to build their physical nature. The result on these two planets was not a gradual disintegration but two massive explosions.

One planet was situated between Venus and Earth and the other between Mars and Jupiter. The debris ripped through the solar system destroying virtually all of the life on all of the remaining planets.

The result of these two explosions was devastating. The remains of these two planets are to be found in the asteroid belt between Mars and Jupiter and in the many millions of asteroids in the outer reaches of the solar system.

A large fragment of one of the planets, the Earth adopted as the moon. The moon is not hollow, it is not an alien construct but it is the cooled down core of the planet between the Earth and Venus. If you look at magma deposits that have cooled following a volcanic eruption you will see that there are large "gas voids" within them. The same is true of the moon – it contains large gas voids.

The other two planets that had decided to leave the solar system did so by moving themselves out of orbit and travelling to a region that is outside of the solar system where they are still slowly disintegrating. The presence of these two planetary "husks" has led to speculation about a Planet X – a tenth planet (often designated the name Nibiru – see Chapter Three). There is no longer a tenth planet; there are nine within our solar system and the remains of two planets just outside of the solar system boundary. In January 2011, astronomers using NASA's "WISE" telescope announced that they had found a new planet beyond the outer Oort Cloud which they believe to be a "gas giant" planet larger then Jupiter. This "new" planet they have provisionally called Tyche (pronounced ty-kee) and is approximately 1,500 times further away from the sun than the Earth is. Two planets slowly disintegrating for 3.9 million years could very well look like a "gas giant".

All of the planets in the solar system changed in some way. Some, such as Venus, shrank in size whilst others, like Jupiter, expanded into a "gas giant". The result being that they all lost their atmospheres and the life that they had built – all were now dead planets.

Except the Earth. The Earth was massively affected by these explosions which rocked the planet on Her equatorial axis. This "rocking" caused the deaths of most of the planets animal life-forms, especially the dinosaurs. Most of the Earth's atmosphere was ripped away and She was very close to joining the other planets and giving up on the "human experiment". However, all of Her hard work at the beginning of Her developing life paid off and she was more resilient than the other planets and so She decided to continue.

Chapter Six

The Development of Human Life

The affects of this solar system-wide disaster were horrendous. Virtually all life in the solar system was destroyed and virtually every planet wiped clean of life.

The Earth managed to hold on, but only just.

The Earth had been rocked on Her equatorial axis causing huge tidal waves and the majority of the animals and proto-humans were washed into the foothills of mountain ranges that spanned east to west across the planet. Over fifty per cent of the atmosphere had been ripped away into space and so many of those who had survived the tsunamis asphyxiated, especially at high altitudes.

Miraculously, many species survived, even if in very small numbers. The atmosphere began to stabilise and the seas receded. Life began again.

Energies were repaired and new energies added to help in reconstruction and the Lady, the Sidhé and the Faerie were hard at work re-building and redesigning plant life as well as introducing new species.

This process of settling and reconstruction took about 100,000 years to complete. When the Earth was satisfied that all was how it should be, She began to look more closely at the development of Her proto-human forms.

The proto-humans that had been developing and evolving on dry land She decided to keep whilst the two different types that had been amphibious She decided to withdraw their template and so they did not exist after this point. This left four types of proto-human varying from Gigantopithicus through Neanderthal to the pygmy. I do not have a scientific name for the fourth proto-human form probably because it has not yet been identified as a separate species.

However, the Earth was not entirely satisfied with these prototypes and asked the NGC to look at and evaluate the proto-human forms that had been developed by the other planets before the solar system-wide disaster wiped out all life.

When this evaluation was complete, the Earth adopted the primary proto-human form that had been developed by Mars. This adoption took place 3.8 million years ago. We know this adopted species as Cro-Magnon Man.

I appreciate that this situation is greatly at odds with the main-stream scientific version of events. However, if you dig under the very thin veneer of scientific propaganda, you will find a very different story.

For a fuller version of scientific cover-ups and deliberate misleading see *The Human Soul*, but, essentially what is found all over the planet are the remains of our direct ancestors – Cro-Magnon Man – evenly distributed everywhere and all dating back as far as about 3.6 million years. Scientific dating techniques are very haphazard in their accuracy but, for once, they seem to have one answer that is very close to the Akashic.

From 3.8 million years ago we have five different types of beings on the planet any of which could have developed into us.

At this stage in human evolution, these proto-humans existed in a state that was more along the lines of how animal life-forms existed. Each proto-human was an individual who was capable of acting individually but mainly acted as a "pack". This was because these proto-humans did not have individual souls but were part of a mass-consciousness.

Each of the five types had their own mass-consciousness and their own energy templates and so did not mate with each other. But they did, however, live fairly compatible lives in that they generally did not try to kill each other off.

Life on Earth From 3.8 Million to 100,000 Years Ago

Drawing from the Akashic, let us try and paint a picture of how life was on Earth for these proto-humans.

The Earth had a vertical rotational axis. This means that there was very little difference between the seasons. The average global temperatures were around plus 6 degrees centigrade and the atmosphere contained a high level of carbon dioxide (see Chapter Twelve for more about the weather).

Temperature variations only occurred as the sun went through its own cycles of energy. When the sun was active, the plus six average temperatures were maintained. When the sun went through its cycles of lower sun spot activity, the temperature could drop by a couple of degrees.

The North Pole was unfrozen whilst the South Pole had snow capped mountains but was otherwise covered in lush vegetation. However, when the sun activity dropped, the South Pole could become frozen and parts of the sea around the South Pole could also freeze over.

This was the only temperature variation that occurred during this whole time period, there were never any "ice ages" where large areas of the planet became covered in ice and snow. Only the South Pole froze and the freezing of the sea never went further north than the tip of South America.

The moon provided for variations in the level of the seas by creating tidal movements which created currents which washed nutrients around the planet's oceans giving abundance to all sea life.

The majority of the Earth's surface was covered in tropical rain forests as well as sub-tropical forests that contained life beyond measure. As each species of plant, bird, insect and animal gradually evolved, every single niche that could support life became filled with species that grew to fill the opportunities that the diversity of habitats presented.

This was a golden age of development and evolution.

Every possible variation on every form of life was tried. If it found a home for itself, it was allowed to stay. The only factor involved in selection is the ability of a species to adapt to its environment, if it could not, it died out and another species took its place – a natural evolution. As far as the proto-humans were concerned, they lived mainly in the rain forests living on fruits which never seemed to stop ripening and on the abundance of animals they took for meat.

Whilst they still had a group-soul, they began to develop more and more into individuals but did not develop sufficiently to be able to accommodate an individual soul.

They had language and learned how to use their hands to fashion tools, both from stone and wood. With these tools they also learned how to build shelters and, for those who lived near a large river or sea, to build boats that allowed them to explore the oceans and live on their abundant life.

In many respects, it was a perfect form of existence. The Earth supplied them fully with all of their needs and they wanted for nothing. Perhaps this was why they were slow to evolve further? This is a question that has never been answered.

Gradually, the Earth became concerned about this situation. Her primary role was to attempt to develop a form of life that was roughly human in form but was able to accommodate a whole soul. This goal did not appear to be any closer. The human proto-types had been allowed to evolve into what they could be but after over three and a half million years, the Earth felt that She was not any closer to meeting Her goal.

Eventually, the Earth asked for help, and for this, She turned to the NGC.

Lemuria

The NGC responded to the Earth's request for help but waited until the sun's activities were at their lowest. After all, the NGC home world is an ice planet and "normal" Earth temperatures made them uncomfortable – see Chapter Three.

There is a great deal of speculation about where the island of Lemuria was located. Many claim that it was in the Pacific Ocean, probably the northern most island in the Hawaiian chain. Others believe it was the South Pole whilst others speculate on South America, South Africa or even Australia.

As far as the Akashic is concerned, the island of Lemuria was an ice island just off the coast of South America – see Illustration Four.

Lemuria was established as a "research" station with the intention of understanding why the human proto-types were so slow in developing sufficiently to a state where they could accommodate a whole soul. It was nothing more than that.

Again, there is a great deal of speculation about the purpose of Lemuria and the activities that went on there. I have to say that I find virtually all of these speculations to be fantasies and the projection of fears rather than any form of reality.

Lemuria was established as a place where the NGC could investigate the life of the proto-humans and was nothing more.

The NGC arrived on Lemuria 98 thousand years ago where they stayed for four thousand years. Lemuria existed for as long as it remained an ice island and then the NGC left.

Unfortunately, when they left, they were no closer to an answer than they were when they first arrived.

So what to do? Did the Earth allow the proto-humans to carry on as they were and develop at their own pace or was there some way in which their development could be accelerated? Whilst time is immaterial, as far as the Universe is concerned, it was a long time for the Earth and She wanted an answer.

Finally, all of those that had been involved in the developments in this solar system met together to discuss the problems with the Earth. The agreed method of approach was to attempt an acceleration of development.

Chapter Seven

The First Humans

Once the decision to bring about an accelerated development of human beings was decided, the next question was where. What was needed was an isolated region of the planet where, if things went wrong, the rest of the human prototypes would not be affected.

The first question was: do the proto-humans want to undergo an accelerated development? After all, freedom of choice is paramount. It was no good the Earth and everyone else connected with developments on Earth, deciding on a course of action if those who would be a fundamental part of those actions did not want to be a part of it.

Although the proto-humans did not have individual souls, they were well aware of their world and their place within it. The proto-humans could be thought of as being a little like a wolf pack. Each individual acted independently but also as part of a larger group with a shared and collective group consciousness. Like wolves, they were highly intelligent and could think for themselves, as individuals, or as part of the "pack" or, more correctly, part of their "clan".

So a question was asked of each of the proto-human groups. Remember there were five distinct proto-human groups at this time, each quite different from the other but each with an equal standing in terms of how the Earth saw her "children". Each group was asked through their collective consciousness and then as individuals.

Whilst a few individuals of each group responded favourably, only one group gave their approval en-mass and that was the Cro-Magnon group.

Had all five groups responded favourably, then all would have undergone accelerated development equally. But, as it turned out, it was only the Cro-Magnon clans who underwent the acceleration process.

Even with this mass acceptance, those who individually rejected the idea were not forced into undergoing the process. Individuals from the other proto-human groups who did choose to undergo this acceleration were allowed to join with the Cro-Magnons.

The rest of the proto-human clans, who had decided not to be a part of this work remained on the planet and developed as they would without any interference.

There are a few isolated survivors from these groups still on the planet today. "Big Foot", Yeti and several other small groups are still alive, living in isolation from the rest of humanity.

The choice of isolation was not made by the Earth, as "modern" man spread out around the planet with our uncaring and unthinking attitudes; we have forced these remaining groups into greater and greater isolation until they have been made virtually extinct.

Atlantis

Eventually it was decided that the continent we know as Atlantis was the most suitable region of the Earth for this experimental acceleration to be carried out. The continent spread across the Atlantic Ocean from Ireland to the Caribbean and contained regions that represented all of the climatic variations on the planet. It was also isolated so that should anything go wrong with the acceleration, the proto-humans on the rest of the Earth would not be affected – see Illustration Four.

With all of these decisions made, Atlantis was established 85,000 years ago.

The first thing that was done was to remove all proto-humans that did not choose to be a part of what was going on. They were moved to another region of the planet of their choosing.

66

Illustration Number Four
A Map of Atlantis

The process of acceleration was this.

By this time, the Cro-Magnon prototypes had bodies that were effectively a fully formed human both in shape and with fully formed internal organs, essentially as we are now. What was lacking were elements of DNA and their inability to accommodate a whole soul. The first thing that was done was to work on the DNA; this allowed the body to become a little lighter in form and in density, a refinement of shape and function.

With the first stage complete, they were more able to draw on a greater part of their group soul; the more group soul they took in, the more their DNA refined. The more the DNA became refined, the more soul they could incorporate and so on in a cycle of development.

Up until this stage, the Cro-Magnon had only three fully formed chakras, as they took on more of their group soul, the other chakras began to grow and develop. The chakras are elements of the soul in the physical body. As their refinement continued, they gradually built to a situation where they had all seven chakras fully formed (see Illustration Five) and stood as complete individuals and fully divorced from their group soul. In other words, an individual being.

At this stage, this individual body form became a new template. They were not fully fledged "Human Beings" yet, but were almost there.

The next stage was entirely different. With a new template, a few representatives of the non-physical races came to Earth. These non-physical souls "borrowed" the template and, by incorporating the energy patterns of the Earth, fashioned a body around their souls.

This is the origin of the Adam and Eve story in the Old Testament – the "first-born" of God coming to Earth and cloaking themselves in the "soil" of the planet.

The immense energies contained within the souls of the non-physical races added further refinements to the body and the DNA which generated a new template.

Finally, the Earth had achieved Her goal and the Creator's question was answered: it was possible to create a physical body that could incorporate the whole of the soul – a Human Being existed.

When this stage was reached, the accelerated Cro-Magnon was further accelerated to fit this new template. This was achieved by detaching them from their group soul and increasing the energy their new individual souls contained until they could match the souls from the non-physical races. This increase in soul energy was carried out by Merlin, the Creator of Energies.

A Human Being is this: a physical body which contains the whole of the soul. The body contains 13 spirals to the DNA (with all of its memories intact – see Chapter Two). There are no chakras: with the whole of the soul incorporated within the physical body, the chakras are superfluous. The body is lighter in density than we are currently used to; our current bodies are more akin to the accelerated Cro-Magnon than to a "true" Human Being. The "normal" life-span of a Human Being is an average of 1,500 years.

Life on Atlantis

How can I describe paradise with the limited vocabulary available?

To start with, I can describe the condition of the planet.

With the Earth fulfilling Her potential, Her consciousness expanded to mirror the work that had been done so She was about 10 per cent larger in diameter than She is currently.

The Earth's rotational axis was vertical and so weather patterns were very stable. The average global temperature was around six degrees centigrade with very little in seasonal differences. The days tended to be hot and dry and, when it did rain, it was gentle and refreshing. Night-time was warm and gentle.

Carbon Dioxide levels were much higher than we currently have in 2011. Carbon dioxide is an extremely important gas which is utilised by every living thing to grow. Human faculties work much better and faster in an atmosphere rich in CO_2 – for details of what is actually happening with our changing weather, see Chapter Twelve.

All other forms of life were abundant. Trees and bushes produced fruit all year round and all animal life flourished.

As to Humans

With the whole soul within the body, we had senses that functioned at much higher levels which were helped by the higher CO_2 levels.

Sight, smell, taste, touch and hearing were at levels we would currently consider impossible.

We communicated psychically with each other and with every living thing. As we psychically communicated with all animals, there was no fear and no mistrust, just friendship and trust.

We could psychically "look" into plants to see what nutritional values they had to us or to animals. We could also "see" what their healing properties were which we used to help heal injured animals.

We did not need healing herbs for ourselves as, with the whole soul within the body we did not become ill and it was extremely rare that we had any kind of accidental injury.

We needed very little in the way of food. We lived on the energy patterns of the Earth's consciousness supplemented by fruit and nuts. However, we did have physical bodies and, every once in a while we needed a protein boost. This we achieved by psychically synthesising sea weed to meet our needs. We did not eat meat.

To travel somewhere we walked as it was such a pleasant thing to do. If we needed to travel great distances we projected our thoughts to where we wanted to be and carried the body along the thought – a process known as translocation. If we needed to, we could also be in two places at the same time, by using the same thought process, we could bi-locate.

The soul is androgynous – neither male nor female and so there were no men or women, just Human Beings. Neither were there any children. The reason for this was not only to do with our androgyny but because we had not thought of a way to divide the soul. Children are born with a small percentage of the soul incorporated within the body. As they grow, more and more of the soul is added until they become adult. At the time of Atlantis, we had no need for this process as the whole of the soul was incorporated into the body as the soul took on Human form – a process called "adult birth".

We saw no need for clothes as the weather was always warm and pleasant. Nor did we build any shelters as we had no need for them, when it came for the time to sleep, we just lay on the ground where we were and slept without any fear of animals.

Our average life-span was in the region of 1,500 years, after which our bodies became a little worn out. However, the process of "dying" was very simple: we just detached the soul from the body and the body rapidly returned to the earth. Once out of body, we could remain around the Earth and communicate freely with everyone who was still "alive". We could also communicate with any other soul. If we chose to begin a new life, we just borrowed the template and constructed a new body.

With the completion of the template for a Human Being, many visitors arrived from the other races. For some it was to marvel at the new creation whilst for others, they came to try out the experience for themselves. In this way, the population steadily grew and all was content and happy.

There were also those of the semi-physical races who came to visit and some wanted to try out this new experience of a full physical body.

As humans, we have a soul who has decided to build for itself a body. The soul, in its natural state, is free-moving and free-acting without any physical density. However, the semi-physical races are a little different. Their body and soul were Created as one, they do not exist separately. For a member of one of the semi-physical races to take on Human form, they needed to find a way of separating the soul from its intrinsic body. This initially proved to be almost impossible and so methods were worked out on Earth to make this process achievable.

A large chamber was built which was lined with crystals. These were crystals made specifically for the purpose. A semi-physical would stand within the crystal chamber and the crystals would be energised in very specific ways. The energy patterns generated were capable of gently stripping away the physical tissue. Once this was achieved, the remaining soul energy could then achieve adult birth. The process

71

could also be reversed but a quantity of the soil from their home planet was needed for the soul to return to its natural semi-physical state.

Experimentation

For several thousand years, this was how Human life was lived. But, life on Earth was an experiment and so began a period where many began to experiment with alterations to the Human body form.

At first, these were experiments carried out to alter the basic Human shape – would it be an advantage to be smaller, to be taller, to have extra limbs? All of these were tried by individuals without altering the basic Human template (see *Planet Earth – The Universe's Experiment*).

Next came the blending of genes. Many Atlanteans took on responsibility for particular animals. They worked with particular animal types in order to understand the ways of life these animals lived. To reflect their interest, these people took into themselves the DNA of particular animal characteristics such as the skin of a zebra, the body shape of a tiger. The most famous of those who worked with animals in this way being the South American "God" Quetzalcoatl who was a tall, blond Atlantean with the skin of a diamond-backed rattle snake.

This was also a time when the idea of male and female was tried. The animal world, as well as the human proto-types, had male and female forms and so many began to investigate building new templates that reflected the choice of the soul to become either male or female. The intention was not to produce children, but to provide variety and choice as Human Beings. Many females did experiment with becoming pregnant to see if it was possible and it was found that it was. However, the problem of dividing the soul had not been worked out and so no children were ever born on Atlantis.

Following these experiments, the state of androgyny was dropped and Human Beings became either male or female with a template for each form but continuing with adult birth.

Problems

We lived in this way for several thousand years but gradually began to notice that we were beginning to experience a few difficulties.

It was noticed that our abilities to translocate were becoming increasingly difficult. Our communication with wild, especially predatory, animals was beginning to become a little haphazard. And, whilst no one had been attacked by predators, we began to become wary of them.

The genetic mixing experiments were becoming more and more bizarre and so we collectively decided to stop all experiments on ourselves until we had worked out where this underlying problem lay.

Very few Humans were aware of the problems we were beginning to notice as life was idyllic. If we couldn't translocate so easily, it did not matter as it was so enjoyable to walk everywhere. If we could no longer sleep on the ground as predatory animals were less friendly towards us, we just built ourselves a nest in the trees (like chimpanzees do).

But, nevertheless, these losses of the higher functions were worrying.

Into this state of worry, there then arose another problem which was far more immediate.

Earth is amazing; there are more forms of life on this planet than the whole of the rest of the Universe combined. The "physical" energies of Earth provide far more scope for expression of life than anywhere else.

For the NGC, this abundance of life was totally fascinating and provided an unlimited source for study and "templates" for life on other worlds. It was one form of life that was being prepared for life on another world that eventually caused the destruction of Atlantis.

The Destruction of Atlantis

We share our Earth with millions of forms of bacteria, all performing necessary tasks which the life on the planet cannot do without. One form of bacteria, which converted one gas into another, was being prepared for transportation to another world and somehow some of the converted bacteria were released into the atmosphere.

The bacteria were in the process of being readied for a planet of semi-physical energies and, whilst the new template was being constructed, the bacteria, which normally lived in the soil, became capable of living on the surface. The modifications that were being made allowed this bacteria to convert oxygen into hydrogen, this was to be its role on its new planet, now imagine the affects such a bacteria could have on Earth where all of its life-forms rely on oxygen in one form or another.

If this modified bacteria had become loose on the planet, all of the oxygen in the body would be converted to hydrogen. This would leave the body as no more then a pile of minerals, not unlike a pillar of salt (the origin of the Sodom and Gomorrah story in the Old Testament).

If the bacteria had become airborne, then all of the oxygen in the atmosphere would have been converted to hydrogen and every living thing on Earth would have died.

To counter the threat of this bacteria, we needed to act very quickly and so we, collectively, decided to destroy the continent.

Even though we were beginning to lose some of our higher psychic functions, we still retained a huge collective psychic potential.

With the assistance of the Earth Herself, we opened up a crack in the Earth's crust that surrounded the continent with volcanoes. Magma poured over Atlantis and completely enveloped it entrapping the bacteria beneath it.

Every Human, every animal and many plants that did not carry this bacteria were moved to safety before the volcanoes erupted and so most were saved. Many, who did carry the bacteria, were buried within the magma to prevent them carrying it to other regions. Those who died in this way just left their bodies and returned to their place of soul origin.

The effects on the planet were devastating.

Chapter Eight

After Atlantis

A world devastated, a dream lost.
The Earth went into shock and shrunk back to the diameter She was before the success of her proto-humans.

The rotational axis shifted and both the North and South Poles froze over, creating the first "ice age" recorded in the Akashic. This was not a gradual freezing but an almost instantaneous icing of most of the northern lands which trapped vegetation and animals under the ice.

South America moved to its current location from where it had been located out in the Pacific Ocean (see Illustration Four).

The Alps and the Pyrenees mountains formed from low foothills, India collided with Tibet making the Himalayas rise to their heights and Africa's Great Rift Valley ripped itself open. Several land masses sank into the ocean whilst several others rose forming new islands.

The devastation was greater than had been caused by the "explosion" of the two planets when they had left the solar system.

Most of the proto-human groups survived but in much reduced numbers and several animal and plant populations were wiped out.
Volcanoes, earthquakes and floods ripped the planet and it was touch and go as to whether the Earth continued.
But, when the dust began to settle, there was hope.

Those who had populated Atlantis moved to other continents, especially South America, West Africa, Egypt and Britain where they found shelter underground in tunnels and caves.

Most of those who remained on the Earth had originated from the semi-physical races and had taken on Human form. The majority of those who were from the non-physical races returned to their place of soul origin.

Sixty five thousand years ago we destroyed a whole continent but then began to pick up the pieces.

Those who had been on Atlantis retained their psychic potential and so set about assisting the Earth in re-building.

In South America, they set about building themselves shelters by expanding and re-shaping underground cave systems that eventually extended to several thousand kilometres.

In Egypt, the same tunnelling work was carried out under the Giza Plateau and the Sphinx was constructed to mark the entrance to the tunnel system. Again these tunnels extended to several thousand kilometres. The face of the Sphinx was originally shaped to match its body, that of a lion, it was changed many thousands of years later by a Pharaoh.

In Britain, a similar tunnel system was built, but on a much smaller scale, under Salisbury Plain with the tunnels' entrance being under West Kennett Long Barrow. The Long Barrow was not there at the time but was built later over the entrance to the tunnels.

Eventually, the volcanoes and earthquakes stopped, the air began to clear and life began to settle into new rhythms.

There was a huge amount of work to be carried out. From a very warm and settled climate there were now very clearly defined seasons with the early winters being particularly harsh with snow covering most of the northern hemisphere for six months of the year.

Most of the remaining proto-humans had moved, or had been moved, to lands around the equator to give them as much chance of survival as possible.

Many species of plants and animals died out as their habitat had changed so radically and so new life needed to be developed to suit the new climate.

Prior to this cataclysm the weather had been extremely stable with the seasons hardly noticeable and all of the plant and animal species were perfectly evolved to live in those conditions. Now, we had a world where winters would extend from the North and South Poles and new plants and animals had to be Created who could survive under the new conditions.

For example; trees were like those found in rain forests and only shed leaves when the individual leaves died. Now, the northern lands needed trees that had strategies to survive a prolonged winter period and so needed to shed all of their leaves in the autumn and become dormant until spring.

The same applied to plants and flowers, all needed to be able to survive winter periods and re-grow when the weather warmed up.

All of this work was carried out by the Humans who remained working in concert with the Lady, the Sidhé and the planet and, in total, it took forty thousand years to complete.

Once all of the work was finished, we had a renewed planet to explore and wonder at.

The weather was not as warm as it had been at the time before and during Atlantis. Instead of there being an average global temperature of around 6 degrees centigrade, it was now closer to 4 degrees (see Chapter Twelve) which is still about 2.5 degrees warmer than we are used to today.

With the planet in a new balance, She also began to expand to a diameter more or less the same as the one we are used to. But, the big question was: should She start again with developing a true Human Being? Human Beings had been successfully developed on Atlantis and so there appeared to be no reason why they could not be developed again. But, did She start again with the proto-humans or did She make use of the template She had built on Atlantis to build a "true" Human Being?

Chapter Nine

New Beginnings

The proto-humans remained on Earth and would be allowed to continue their own development in their own time and in their own ways without interference from anyone.

The Earth decided that the Human Being template would be re-used but instead of isolating the new Humans to a single continent, they would be spread out across the planet's surface in small communities where they could fully explore different climates and different ways of life but all charged with the same task – why did we begin to lose our higher psychic functions on Atlantis?

To fulfil this exploration, six different regions were chosen and all were isolated from the clans of the proto-humans so that contact would be kept to the minimum. This "new beginning" was put into action 20,000 years ago.

These six regions were:

South America – particularly Mexico, Guatemala and Belize.

Mesopotamia – parts of the regions we now know as Southern Turkey, Syria, Iran and Iraq down to the Persian Gulf.

Egypt – most of the Red Sea coastline and parts of Ethiopia.

Northern Europe – Britain, Ireland and Northern France.

Tibet – the whole of the newly raised Tibetan Plateau.

Southern Greece – a region that stretched from Athene to Crete (most of this area was destroyed by a later earthquake and no longer exists).

By locating in these regions, it was hoped that all of the new life could be explored and understood as well as find the answer to our most pressing question.

Each of the regional groups began exploring their renewed environment, most just living within nature whilst others, particularly South America and Southern Iran/Iraq (ancient Sumeria) adopted what we would describe as a "scientific" approach.
Those who returned to the Earth adopted the template of a full Human Being that had been developed on Atlantis and some even recreated their bodies with genes added from particular animal groups. These Human/animal mixtures became the animal-headed "Gods" of later mythologies.

Life on Earth was very similar to how life had been lived on Atlantis; a Paradise where we had our full psychic capabilities. If we wished to travel around the planet to visit the other groups, we translocated. If we wanted to know what properties a particular plant had, we "asked" it psychically. Nothing on this new world was closed to us.
Those who had taken on a "scientific" role developed telescopes and microscopes. A great deal of evidence for this has been archaeologically uncovered but remains largely secret as these kinds of discoveries do not fit into the current scientific model of our history.
This hiding of true human history is very common and our schools and universities teach a form of propaganda rather than historical truth.

The Pyramids
Even in this paradise, we began to encounter problems with maintaining our higher psychic functions.
Our average life span was around 1,500 years and as these reductions in capabilities happened over a period of a few hundred years, they were not immediately noticed or even seen as a particular problem.

However, the problems were sufficiently worrying to look for solutions.

The problem seemed to be that the whole of the soul could not be fully accommodated within the Human body for a full life span. This was not some kind of partial "death" that was being experienced but the partial "leakage" of some of the soul's higher energy frequencies out of the body which created a kind of "aura" around the body but were not consciously available.

Several forms of investigation were tried to see if the problem could be overcome but none seemed to present any kind of answer.

Eventually, we decided to attempt to re-merge these higher frequencies back into the body. In order to achieve this, we built the Great Pyramid on the Giza Plateau in Egypt.

The reason for building a pyramid was to make use of the energy patterns that square pyramids generate. If you construct a square pyramid, you will find that the shape itself generates and concentrates energies at a point about one third of its height up from the base. By enhancing these natural energy concentrations, the soul could be fully re-merged back into the body. This is why the so-called "King's Chamber" is located where it is – it is at this point of greatest energy concentration.

The chambers that have been found within the Great Pyramid are only half of the number of chambers that were built. The Queen's Chamber and the King's Chamber have mirror images within the pyramid that have not yet been "officially" found.

The pyramids were constructed psychically. A group of people collected together and created a collective focussed thought in the limestone quarry from where the stones were taken. This "group thought" cut through the solid rock to form individual blocks of stone perfectly shaped for their locations.

Once the stones were cut to shape, they were psychically transported and then lifted into position on the pyramid. When in place, the stones would be "rubbed" together, again psychically, so that there was always a perfect fit between them.

Above the King's Chamber are the so-called "air vents", chambers which contain carefully cut and placed stones which form a pattern known as a "djed" pillar. These djed pillars are not part of some kind of air conditioning system but are energy accumulators and reflectors.

Into the King's Chamber was psychically transported a granite "box" that has become erroneously called the sarcophagus.

There are many theories about how the pyramids were built; virtually all of them ignore a psychic means of construction. There have been numerous attempts to build half-scale replicas of the Great Pyramid using these construction theories – none of them work. Some aspects of the theories have been shown to work; such as the use of greased slides to move massive stone blocks as the ancient Egyptians did not have use of the wheel. With the success of this extremely small part of their theories shown to have some benefit, the archaeologists then claim that the whole of their theory is correct even though all other aspects have been proven not to work.

It is worth looking at some aspects of these theories just to show that the title of "Pyramidiot" belongs more to the Egyptologists than those who put forwards "alternative" theories.

The only form of metal found from ancient Egypt is copper and the Egyptologists claim that stone cutting tools were made from this metal.

Copper tools cannot cut solid rock – every attempt to show that they can has failed. Copper tools cannot even shape solid rock once it has been cut.

The sarcophagus in the King's Chamber is made from an extremely hard form of granite. The sarcophagus is about 2.4m x 1m (8ft x 3ft) and about 0.8m high (about 2ft 7ins) and the whole of the inside of this huge block has been hollowed out. Copper tools cannot even scratch this type of granite let along cut. Attempts were made to cut a small version of the sarcophagus using the latest diamond cutters and laser cutters. Neither of these techniques could cut through the granite without shattering it.

The setting out of the Great Pyramid, on its base, is so accurate and so perfectly aligned that we could not set it out as accurately even using the latest technology.

The theory that the cut stones were moved into position by using greased slides sitting on top of sand ramps has also been studied in detail.

It is possible to move very large blocks of cut stone by sliding them over greased timber slides providing you have enough man-power to pull the weight of the blocks. However, to build a sand ramp that reached to the top of the pyramid is a non-starter. The sides of the pyramid slope inwards from its base which means that the ramp has to increase in width as it climbs up the pyramid walls. This increasing width puts enormous pressure on the ramp below which is almost certain to cause a collapse of the ramp. It could be possible to make a stable ramp but the volume of sand needed to build it is greater than the volume of sand available in the surrounding landscape even if the sand was transported several miles. Although this region of Egypt looks like desert it is, in fact, a limestone plateau with only a thin cover of sand.

Then there is of course the theory that the Pyramid was a tomb.

When archaeologists first blew their way into the Pyramid and made their way to the King's Chamber, the sarcophagus was full of a grey powder and not a body. In other words, no burials were ever carried out in the Pyramid itself. There was one body buried at the base of the Pyramid but even the archaeologists describe this as a "break-in burial" made some time after the Pyramid was finished and had nothing to do with the Pyramid at all.

Lastly, of course is the age of the Pyramid.

Egyptologists have dated the Great Pyramid to about 4,000 years ago. This date was arrived at when an archaeologist, who was digging *outside* of the Pyramid, uncovered a pottery shard which was dated to that time. That is it, there seems to be no other way in which the "official" dating for the Pyramid has been arrived at.

There are a number of pyramids dotted around Egypt. All of them are more crudely built than the Great Pyramid on the Giza Plateau and all of them have been dated as being built *after* the Great Pyramid. In other words, the later pyramids were not prototypes for the Great Pyramid with the Pyramid being the pinnacle of the techniques learned by building the others. The Great Pyramid pre-dates all of the others.

The Akashic records the date for the Pyramid's building as 18,000 years ago.

Author's Note: the scientific testing of their theories I have given here has been collected from various journals and books over the years and so I cannot give a list of the publications or their dates but the information given is accurate.

To return to the purpose for which the Great Pyramid was built.

The Great Pyramid was finished with smooth white limestone which shone brightly in the sun. Half way up each corner was positioned a quartz crystal about 1.8m (6ft) tall. On the very top, the pyramidion, was positioned a crystal that was over 2.4m (8ft) tall. These giant crystals gathered together huge amounts of energy which were focused, through the so-called "star shafts", into the King's Chamber.

If you were someone who wished to re-merge the higher frequencies of the soul back into the body you entered the Pyramid and made your way to the Queen's Chamber. This was used as an ante chamber, somewhere where you could prepare yourself. Once ready, you entered into the King's Chamber where you created a specific sound. This sound was both psychic as well as verbal. This sound generated a standing wave frequency which resonated with all of the massive energies contained within the King's chamber and this combination of energies increased your own vibrations so that the whole of the soul would re-merge back into the body.

This is the only purpose for which the Great Pyramid was built.

The grey powder found in the sarcophagus was, at first, dismissed as dust but it is now known that the powder was a form of alchemically altered gold – known as "shew bread" or "star-fire bread". Ingesting this substance is known to increase someone's psychic abilities.

Five of the six regions that had been re-settled by Human Beings followed suit and built their own Pyramids for the same purpose.
I have only focussed on the Egyptian Pyramid as it is the one best known to people and, because it is best known, it is assumed that Egypt was the greatest of these ancient settlements. This is not true. The buildings and work carried out in South America is far greater than anything found in Egypt and this is yet to be uncovered by archaeologists.

Incidentally, the reason why the Egyptian Great Pyramid is now stepped on the outside is because the smooth limestone blocks that originally faced it were scavenged to build some of the older buildings in Cairo.

Pyramids were built in five of the six re-settled regions; the sixth region adopted a different approach.
The primary energy intake point onto the planet is in Southern Britain and so the region of Northern France, Britain and Ireland had maintained their higher psychic functions for longer. Also, because there was a huge clean energy source available, the construction of pyramids was unnecessary as other forms could be used to concentrate energy frequencies as happened in the King's Chamber.

The Earth has two energies. The first is Her own soul or consciousness energy whilst the second is the energy She supplies to sustain the life She created. This "life energy" is distributed around the planet by an energy grid we have come to know as "ley lines". To assist and enhance the ley line energy, the planet draws on a source of universal energy.

This universal energy was put into place at the start of the development of our solar system as a means of providing as much energy as was necessary to bring about our "experiment" in physical life. All of the planets of the solar system had access to this energy flow, including the Earth. This universal energy flow arrives on the planet at what is now Silbury Hill in Wiltshire.

18,000 years ago, the English Channel did not exist and Britain and Ireland were only separated by a tidal river so they were, effectively, one land.

The huge energies that came into Silbury Hill meant that instead of building a pyramid, this region built Stonehenge to perform the same function. This was the earliest development at Stonehenge, the later Trilothon structures were added at a later date – see below.

Finding Answers

By the time the Great Pyramid was built, we knew what the problem was; we knew why we were losing some of the higher aspects of the soul. The reason was this: in order to generate and nurture "physical" life, the Earth generated an energy frequency of 7.56 Hz (7.56 cycles per second). This base-note frequency coalesced the energies connected with the planet into "physical" form. This base-note frequency was fine for animal and plant life but was too low for the much higher frequencies needed to fit the whole of the soul into the Human body. This is why the pyramids were required; they increased and raised the body's frequency to a point where the soul could re-merge. The problem was that nobody could work out just what the Earth's base-note frequency needed to be raised to.

This point about frequency was a critical problem. If the frequency was not raised enough, Humans would still encounter the same problem but over a longer period. If the frequency was raised too high, it could destroy animal and plant life and nobody wanted that to happen.

The problem with Earth is that it is the most beautiful planet in the Universe with more forms of life than the rest of the Universe combined. It is, therefore, an extremely distracting place to live. How can you concentrate on finding this one answer when everywhere you look there is a new life-form to distract you especially if you can convince yourself that this new life-form might help to find the answer.

So the vigour with which we pursued an answer became a little slowed. Also, we were beginning to slow down even more; the longer we stayed on the planet, the more of the higher psychic functions we lost.

We did, however decide to take one major radical step to see if it could produce a solution.

Up until this stage, we had continued with the process of "adult birth"; we did not have any children. Given that the slowing of the higher psychic functions showed that the soul could be divided we, collectively, decided to try giving birth to children. It was hoped that the children would "grow" into their full soul and solve the problem. The first Human child was born 16,000 years ago.

This birth process proved to be only moderately successful and only about thirty per cent of the Human population adopted it. However, it was realised how special children are and the process was continued just for the pleasure of sharing the world with children.

This might seem as though it was taking a long time for things to happen. After all, we had now been on Earth for 4,000 years and we seemed to be no further forwards.

It must be remembered that the majority of the souls who had taken on Human form were from the non-physical races to whom time is immaterial. Also, those who were from the semi-physical races were used to extremely long time-spans and so 4,000 years did not appear to be a very long time. In addition, with an average life-span of 1,500 years, we had only been on Earth for just over two generations.

In addition, our higher psychic functions were slowly being eroded and this also slowed down our ability to investigate. In addition, our loss of higher psychic functions was accelerating and this acceleration seemed to be connected to the shift in the Earth's rotational axis that had occurred at the end of Atlantis. In fact, this accelerated slowing down brought with it its own set of problems.

Chapter Ten

Language and Writing

U p to about 16,000 years ago we were able to maintain our abilities to communicate psychically – we did not use spoken or written language. Our ability to remember the results of our investigations and to freely access the Akashic meant that nothing was physically recorded.

As we began to lose these higher functions, we found we needed to find a way of recording information. For this purpose, we developed "hieroglyphs".

We are used to seeing the forms of hieroglyphs in South America and Egypt but these are forms that occurred at a later time. The original forms of hieroglyphs were not written or painted but were cut into stone.

These original hieroglyphs were a form of psychic "aide memoire". The way they were formed was by psychically imprinting your thoughts into the stone itself, a kind of psychic "stone carving" which was not read as a language but the image was "read" by focusing your thoughts on the carving and the memories stored within it would be psychically transferred directly into the brain.

For example, the whole of the base of the Great Pyramid was psychically "carved" in this way to remind people how to use the Pyramid. All of these particular carvings were lost when the limestone facing stones to the Pyramid were stripped for building material in later times.

Most of the original forms of hieroglyphs carved into stone in South America have also been lost. The carved hieroglyphs that have been found in recent years are more along the lines of a written language.

As we continued our slow loss of psychic functions, we gradually also lost the ability to carve and read these kinds of hieroglyphs and so, about 12,000 years ago, we began to develop a more written form of language.

This first "root" written language was based on the electrical impulses that flow up and down the spine and looked more like a modern "bar code" than writing. However, this first written form is the basis for all other written forms of language especially Cuneiform, Ogham and Runes.

Along with the need to develop writing, came the need to develop spoken language.

Psychic communication allows you to directly transfer information to another person – not only meaning but sensory information is transferred as well. As we lost our ability to communicate in this way, we developed a spoken language to be able to fulfil some of these lost functions.

There was a single spoken language developed originally but, as each of the six groups became more isolated, they developed their own regional variations.

The need to develop language, both spoken and written, reflected how far we had fallen from our origins. In just 8,000 years we had gone from fully psychic beings to ones who had lost many of the original psychic capabilities and our life expectancy had dropped from an average of 1,500 years to an average of 500 years.

But life on Earth was still such an amazing adventure that we hardly noticed the loss.

The Formation of a "Priesthood"

Despite this general loss of higher functions, there were those who tried to maintain their whole souls within the body. Unfortunately, the number of people to do this was dropping. In order that the knowledge was not lost, some people took on the role of remembering how to use the Pyramids.

To activate the King's Chamber, a sound sequence was required and this sound sequence came to be known as "The Keys of Enoch". These sound sequences were extremely important as they triggered reverberations and standing wave responses within the King's Chamber which re-merged the soul back into the body. If the knowledge of these sounds was lost, the Pyramids could not be used and we would not have a way to re-gain our lost abilities.

Really speaking, these "Keepers of the Keys of Enoch" were the first form of a secret society or "priesthood" – those who retained a certain type of knowledge which was not generally available to everyone.

In Egypt, a tradition was begun where someone who chose to regain their higher psychic functions was educated by the Priests in how to regain and retain these faculties and, eventually, became known as Pharaoh. In other traditions, in the other five regions, those who retained this higher knowledge became known as Kings.

The original function of the Pharaoh or King was to be someone who could access full knowledge of who and what we are and lead us to regaining the ability to re-merge the whole soul back into the body.

The method of remembering knowledge was slightly different in Britain. Silbury Hill still performed its energy intake function to provide the energy boost needed but the memory of how to use Stonehenge was recorded in stones.

Between 10,000 and 7,000 years ago, the stone structures that make up the original six circles to Avebury were gradually built. Instead of using hieroglyphs, as elsewhere, the stone avenues and circles of Avebury had the necessary knowledge psychically imprinted into them. In this way, the stones were "read" in a process similar to psychometry.

Essentially, those who wished to re-merge the whole soul back into the body "showered" themselves in the energy of Silbury then progressed through each of the Avebury circles en-route to the energy available at the Stonehenge circles.

The "hill" at Silbury was not built until about 7,000 years ago and acts as an "accumulator" – a battery - to give a large energy boost to those who wished to use it.

Eventually, by about 8,000 years ago, we had fallen so far from our original state that we needed to find a new approach.

Also at this time, we were temporarily cut off from the rest of the Universe for reasons that we did not learn for some time (see Chapter Eleven).

The Human Plan

As far as the Human population and the Earth were concerned, we were in dire straights.

The goal of a complete Human Being had been again met but now seemed to be slipping away. It was known that the Earth's own energy frequencies were causing problems in our ability to maintain the whole soul within the physical body and this seemed to be further exacerbated by the planet's rotational "wobble" that had existed since the destruction of Atlantis. We could maintain the whole soul within the body for a short time after adult birth and we could even maintain that state for an equally short time once a child had reached puberty. But the time we were able to maintain this state was becoming less and less and we were no closer to answering the question of what the Earth needed to change Her base-note frequency to.

But what to do? What new approach did we need to adopt to find the answer?

Given we had been mysteriously cut off from the rest of the Universe and could not obtain any advice from that direction; we decided to discuss it amongst ourselves. By this I mean that all of the souls who were in Human form needed to get together to work out an answer.

The only way in which this kind of gathering could work is if we left our bodies behind and re-merged the whole soul whilst out of body. Ninety per cent of all six groups underwent this process; that is, they physically died. The remaining 10 per cent elected to remain physical to look after crops and flocks whilst this soul-level conference took place.

What we collectively came up with is recorded within the Akashic as "The Human Plan".

The Plan itself is quite simple: using the experience we had gained from being able to produce children – dividing the soul – we would divide the soul into two. The greatest "quantity" of soul energy would form the "Higher Self" – about 75 per cent of the total soul – whilst the remaining 25 per cent would inhabit a physical body which had been built under the direction of the Higher Self. The "physical self" would live a lifetime experiencing all that the Earth had to offer. At the end of a particular lifetime, the "physical" aspect of the soul would re-merge with the "Higher" aspect to review the knowledge gained from the experiences undergone in the recently finished life. With this review completed, the Higher Self and the physical aspect of the soul would carefully plan the next lifetime, building into it a new set of experiences.

This is a process we have come to know as "reincarnation". Each new incarnation added to our personal and collective knowledge. This gathering of knowledge we know by a Sanskrit word: "Karma".

This is all that the word Karma actually means – knowledge – it does not mean debt, nor does it mean a burden, nor does it mean that we have had something "heavy" imposed upon us; it just means knowledge.

Also incorporated into the physical body were seven energy centres we commonly know as the "Chakras". These seven energy points are located in exactly the same locations within the body for everyone (see Illustration Five). These chakras are aspects of the Higher self made physical. If we strayed from our chosen path in life, the Higher Self would deplete the energies of one, or more, of the chakras and we would begin the symptoms of an illness (for a full explanation of this process see *Everything You Always Wanted to Know About Your Body* and *The Sequel to Everything*). This is all that an illness is, it is a hint from the Higher Self to tell the Physical Self that we have strayed off our chosen path and we need to correct our actions to re-steer our lives into the correct direction.

If we ignored the symptoms of illness – the promptings of the Higher Self – we died, returned to the Higher Self to plan how to correct where

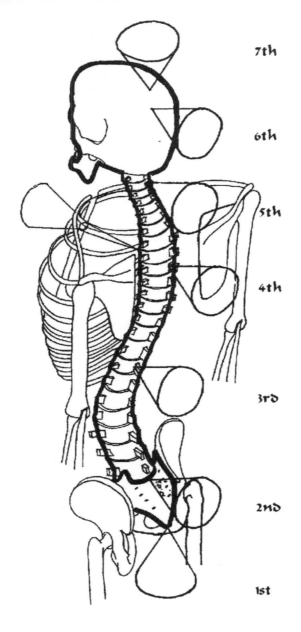

7th

6th

5th

4th

3rd

2nd

1st

Illustration Number Five
The Seven Primary Chakras

94

we went wrong in our lives. If we paid attention to the symptoms of illness, and corrected our actions, the symptoms of illness disappeared and we were able to carry on.

We put The Human Plan into action 7,000 years ago and have been living our lives this way ever since. This division of the soul meant that we are not fulfilling our true potential but investigating how we could arrive at a place where we could re-merge the soul back into the physical body.

In our divided soul state, the Earth considers the physical aspect to be "sub-human" and she allowed us 7,000 years to return to our full Human Being state.

This is where we currently are; at the end of this 7,000 year period and, as we move into 2012, we must have either re-merged the soul or we must leave the planet and return to our place of soul origin.

Chapter Eleven

Interference

Instigating The Human Plan turned out to be a huge success. We learned a great deal about the Earth, and our place within it, very rapidly. However, we could not decide on the most crucial question of all: to what frequency did the Earth need to raise Her energies in order for us to be able to re-merge the soul into the physical body and continue to live as full Human Beings?

This earth and this solar system are totally unique. Throughout the whole of Creation, there is nowhere like our solar system. As such, we have no guidance and no reference points against which to judge our progress in this "experiment" we call human life and so, when unusual events begin to happen, it takes a long time to realise that they are not a natural part of life on Earth. This is especially true with the arrival of new energies about 2,400 years ago.

The Fourteenth Faction

You will have seen from Chapter Two that we are not the only universe that exists. There are currently eleven universes in total each exploring a Thought of the Creator.

Some of the universes are new whilst others are approaching the end of their life; having reached the answer to their originating Thought. One such universe, which was nearing its process of collapse and return to the Creator, was next to ours.

Our Universe explores the concept of complete freedom of choice – every soul within this Universe has the absolute freedom to choose their actions; the only limiting factor is that nobody can act in such a way as to remove the freedom of choice of another. An adjacent universe was exploring the exact opposite Thought – what would happen if every soul within a universe had the absolute freedom to remove freedom of choice? Needless to say, it was a chaotic universe which lasted less than half the time that our Universe has been in existence.

This is where the strangeness of time begins to show itself. Obviously I can only give time references as they relate to Earth and this is why some events recorded within the Akashic seem to be unsynchronised with Earth time frames.

Three million, six hundred thousand years ago, just as we were recovering from the solar system-wide disaster of two planets "exploding" and the Earth was in the process of adopting Cro-Magnon Man from Mars, an event occurred out in the Universe which would have profound affects on life on Earth and how we lived our karmic lifetimes under The Human Plan.

In Universal time, this event took place 3.6 million years ago. In Earth time, it coincided with the shutting down of the solar system 8,000 years ago. Strange stuff time!

Regardless of time-frames, what happened was this.

Beings from this adjacent universe were looking for ways in which they could prolong their existence. They knew that their universe had begun the process of collapse and return to the Creator as they could read the Akashic of their universe. What they did was to indentify the location of another universe and find a way of breaking out of their universe and into the other. Unfortunately for us, this adjacent Universe was ours.

Essentially, these beings from the other universe created what our cosmologists would call a "wormhole". This is an open ended "tube" of energy that allows for travel in both directions. One end of the wormhole was in their universe and the other opened into ours.

The energy of the wormhole breaking through created a huge explosion, in our Universe, and 30,000 souls on their way to Earth were caught in the blast.

This blast of energy acted a little like radiation on these 30,000 souls and they became contaminated with the energies of the other universe. In other words, these 30,000 souls became capable of removing freedom of choice. In a Universe that is constructed around the energies of absolute freedom of choice, souls capable of *removing* freedom of choice were a disaster.

This was the reason why our solar system was temporarily isolated from the rest of the Universe 8,000 years ago. The Thirteen attempted to protect all of the physical forms of life developing in our solar system from being destroyed by the beings from this other universe.

The Akashic records the name of these beings that came from another universe as The Fourteenth Faction (I'll refer to them as the Fourteen). The Fourteen entered our Universe with the intention of "stealing" energies that they hoped they could use to maintain their position within their own universe and stop them returning back to the Creator.

In order to carry out their intended task, they brought with them what can only be described as "mining machinery". The use of this machinery allowed them to "mine" the energies of our Universe and convert the frequencies to those that were compatible with their own universe.

I am only going to spend a brief time describing the actions and activities of the Fourteen as I have covered this more fully in my previous two books *Planet Earth - The Universe's Experiment* and *The Universal Soul.*

Essentially, the Fourteen were very successful at what they came here to do. Eventually, they destroyed about one quarter of the energy resources of this Universe. Fortunately, this "dead zone" is far away from our galaxy.

The beings who maintain the balance of energies within our Universe – The Thirteen – had extreme difficulty dealing with the Fourteen as the energy patterns of the Fourteen do not exist within our Universe. How can you fight something when you do not even have the ability to defend yourself let alone destroy your "attackers"?

Eventually, The Thirteen were successful and the Fourteen have been totally removed from this Universe.

To return to the affects of the Fourteen energies on Earth.

3.6 million years ago, 30,000 souls were contaminated by these energies whilst on their way to Earth. However, these 30,000 disappeared for quite some time – the Akashic does not record what happened to them in the period immediately after the wormhole was opened.

The first sign we saw on Earth of someone making use of the ability to remove freedom of choice was about 2,400 years ago with the arrival of Alexander the Great.

By the time Alexander arrived, we had been working within The Human Plan for about five and a half thousand years and were making steady progress. Many karmic lifetimes had been lived and we were accumulating a great deal of knowledge about ourselves and about the Earth. As we lived these lifetimes, we did occasionally have disputes with neighbours over issues like land or water rights which did, sometimes, lead to violence. However, these skirmishes were very local to where the problem arose but, with the arrival of someone who could remove freedom of choice, Alexander had bigger ideas and became the first person to kill and conquer for the sake of bringing power and empire to themselves.

Alexander was closely followed by those who made use of these Fourteen energies to build the Roman Empire.

Immediately following the Roman Empire we have an organisation that has done more than any other to destroy The Human Plan – the Vatican.

The Vatican has consistently made use of the ability to remove freedom of choice and has done so by destroying every document that contradicted their dogma and butchered every person who stood in their way. For the last 1,600 years the Vatican has done everything in its power to control humanity and prevent us from understanding the truth about ourselves.

Several other individuals have also made use of the Fourteen energies they were contaminated with which has resulted in either personal empires or empires under the control of a particular country but, gradually, these energies have faded and with the total removal of the Fourteen out of our Universe in March 2002, nobody is able to draw on these frequencies and remove freedom of choice.

We will leave the influence of the Fourteen there for now as their energy patterns have been totally destroyed and can no longer have any influence on Earth. However, there are two things connected with the Fourteen which are worth noting.

Firstly, although 30,000 souls were contaminated by these bizarre energies, they were not forced into making use of them. The energies did not, of themselves, force souls to make use of them. The vast majority of these 30,000 exercised their freedom of choice to totally reject these energies. Those who did make use of the Fourteen energies did so as a matter of choice. In other words, they chose to attempt to take control over others; an action which the Universe totally condemns as it breaks the fundamental energy patterns of this Universe – every soul has the absolute right to choose their own actions what a soul cannot do is to act in such a way as to remove the choice of others.

Secondly, the beings that came from the other universe were humanoid in form but their physiology and physical appearance was very close to that of a reptile.

If you were psychic, and approached one of those who had chosen to make use of the Fourteen energies, then the overwhelming impression that you would gain is that the person in front of you was a reptile hiding behind a human façade.

The Velon

The Velon race was briefly described in Chapter Three. The Velon have a very strange approach to Earth, believing that it should be their planet. The reasons for their belief are complex and I do not wish to repeat the problems they have caused on Earth over the past 300 years as that has been fully covered by *The Human Soul, Project Human Extinction* and *The Annunaki Plan? or The Human Plan?* so there is no need to repeat the information. What I would like to do here is to bring up to date the information in those previously published books.

The Velon have been effectively "shunned" by this Universe because of their activities on and around Earth. A proportion of the Velon have managed to avoid this expulsion and have found a way of remaining within this Universe. Trying to track down their exact numbers and locations has proven to be very difficult as they adopt a great many disguises and are adept at hiding by travelling backwards in time.

There would appear to be a few hundred Velon who are on the planet's surface. Some, a very few, have managed to take on human form but the majority are located on military bases such as the infamous Area 51 where they are frequently known as "Tall White Nordics". There is a reason for this name which has nothing to do with Velon appearance – see Chapter Thirteen for an explanation. Most of the Velon who are on the planet are in deep underground secret military bases and use their psychic capabilities to attack people.

The vast majority of the remaining Velon, about 3.5 million, are located in ships just outside of our solar system energy "bubble" (see Illustration Three). The guardians of the Earth and solar system have denied them access to the solar system and so they remain outside. However, the Velon influence is spread far and wide through the military and the so-called "Elite" and many attempts have been made by people to form openings in the solar system "bubble" in an attempt to allow the Velon access.

Two examples of this are the "Norwegian Spiral" that appeared over Tromsø in Norway on December the 9th 2009. The "spiral in the sky" was generated by the nearby HAARP station and was an attempt to open a "portal" to allow the Velon access.

The other is the construction of the Hadron Accelerator in the Cerne complex on the Swiss/French border. Firing up the Accelerator was a deliberate attempt to form a "black hole" within the solar system.
Both of these attempts failed.

However, the most unpleasant attempt to enter the solar system was made by the Velon and was directly targeted against individual people.

For many years, two of the Velon races, the Annunaki and the Hathor, have been seducing people into believing that all of the problems associated with the change we are undergoing can be solved by them. There has been an unbelievable amount of channelled information bombarded at people stating that organisations such as The Great White Brotherhood, The Galactic Federation and Ashtar Command along with hundreds of "angels" are here to transport us away from Earth to an unspecified location where we would be "ascended to a 5th dimension". Unfortunately, millions of people have fallen for this fantasy. These people have become so enraptured by these channelled messages that they have been prepared to give up virtually anything to ensure that they were one of the "chosen ones".
The real purpose to the Annunaki/Hathor "grooming" these people was revealed on Christmas Eve 2010. What the Velon attempted to do on Christmas Eve was to enact 3.5 million "walkins".
A "walkin" is a situation where the soul is forcibly ejected from the body and another soul "walks in" to the vacated body and takes it over. In other words, the Velon attempted what amounts to mass murder to 3.5 million humans on Christmas Eve 2010. Fortunately, those who guard the Earth rapidly became aware of the Annunaki/Hathor plans and the "walkin" process was stopped without any human souls being lost.
Most of these 3.5 million people are now aware, on one level or another, that they had been conned by the Annunaki/Hathor and have begun to reject the Velon fantasy stories which is diminishing the Velon's capabilities to cause further disruption to our process of completion.

Whilst it could be argued that, as humans, we had little defence against those who chose to make use of the energies of the Fourteenth Faction; those energies were fully removed from Earth in 2002.

Since then, the number of people who have fallen for the shenanigans of the Velon/Annunaki/Hathor is staggering. In recent years, we have had a growing culture of people looking for a quick fix to solve their problems. There seem to be a growing number of people who do not wish to take any kind of responsibility for resolving the problems they have generated in their lives and the Velon ruthlessly exploited the gullibility of such people.

To fulfil our potential, and undergo our process of re-merging the soul back into the body, nobody is going to step in and do the work for us. We are on our own in this, both collectively and individually. If you have chosen to re-merge the soul back into the physical; it will only happen if you take responsibility for yourself.

Chapter Twelve

Current Planetary Changes

As we undergo a shift in consciousness, so does the Earth. There are many changes occurring on many levels and some of these are being used as a means of trying to slow down our process of change by distracting our attention by generating fear amongst the population.

You do not need to have access to the Akashic to gain the truth about this propagandised fear mongering – you just have to open your eyes and pay attention. Most of what follows in this chapter has been researched just by reading information together with taking an interest in what is actually happening in the world.

I am not going to provide a bibliography for the sources of this material; if you disagree with what is contained here, I suggest you go and investigate it for yourself.

International Terrorism

Strictly speaking, this does not have anything to do with planetary changes but it does impact on people. By making us believe that there are terrorist organisations, such as al-Qaeda, it is engendering widespread fear and fear distracts us from our movement for change.

To understand what terrorism is really all about, you need to look at its roots.

When the country of Israel was officially formed at Britain's recommendation in 1948 as an apology for the Nazi concentration camps from World War Two, Israel very quickly began to attempt to annexe Palestine. Realising their mistake, the British government set up an organisation to counter the Israeli attempt at genocide. This organisation was made up of fundamentalist Muslims, known as Wahabi Muslims, and they chose the name of al-Qaeda.

When things temporarily settled down in Palestine, the British had no further use for al-Qaeda and it went underground. However, when Russia invaded Afghanistan in the 1980's, control of al-Qaeda passed from British hands to the CIA.

When asked on camera what the one time Home Secretary, Robin Cook, knew of al-Qaeda, he stated that the only organisation of that name he knew of was a list of CIA "assets" listed on his computer.

Taking pity on the plight of the Afghani's, the son of a Saudi Arabian billionaire, Osama Bin Laden, began making financial contributions to al-Qaeda. As Bin Laden's involvement grew, he became personally involved in Afghanistan.

The CIA trained, armed and financed al-Qaeda to help their struggle against the Russian invasion. In exchange for their assistance, the CIA took payment in heroin. The head of the CIA at the time, George Bush snr approved the importation of drugs by the CIA and the drugs were sold on the streets of America to raise funds for CIA "black operations" (black operations is the name given to the activities of the CIA that are not accountable to the US Congress).

When George Bush snr retired as American President, the White House confirmed that he went to work for a company wholly owned by the Bin Laden family.

If we turn to Europe in the 1970's we find the Bader Meinhoff Gang who carried out acts of terrorism mainly against Germany. It turns out that the Gang was made up of NATO troops and was financed through NATO.

During the 1980's we had a number of terrorist attacks on the British mainland that were blamed on the IRA. It turns out that several of these attacks were British troops on live ammunition training exercises.

On September 11th 2001, the World Trade Centre in New York had two planes flown into the twin towers, supposedly flown by al-Qaeda operatives. The buildings could not possibly collapse in the way in which they did without assistance from explosives – ask any architect or engineer. When the basements of the towers were finally cleared six weeks later, the salvagers found hot molten metal that was radioactive. The only way in which this could have happened is by attaching small thermo-nuclear charges to the basement steel columns. Thermo-nuclear charges are only available to the military.

There are also literally hundreds of other known facts about the destruction of the Twin Towers and all of them point to the CIA carrying out the attacks.

In London on the 7th of July 2005, a number of bombs were detonated on busses and on the underground. Later on that year, the SIS (formally MI6) admitted on the BBC evening news that "a rogue cell within the SIS had recruited, trained and armed the bombers". I know this is totally correct as I watched the news programme live. This statement by the SIS was not repeated on the TV news nor was it reported in any newspaper.

So really, the question has to be – Who are the terrorists? The very clear answer is our own governments. As to the reasons why governments would carry out these atrocities on their own electorate; see *Project Human Extinction – The Ultimate Conspiracy.*

Bio Fuels and Population

We touched briefly on the problems with bio fuels in Chapter Three and I am very glad to say that The Friends of the Earth began a campaign in early 2011 to highlight the problems these crops cause.

Having spoken personally with someone who worked in oil exploration for over 20 years, I think it fair to say that there is no oil shortage; in fact the world is currently awash with oil. The only reason why oil prices have risen in recent years is the oil cartels increasing their profits. I am not a fan of oil; I believe that we should have had Tesla's "free energy" system which is the only *real* solution to our energy needs.

Wind power is a complete failure both on the damage it does to the environment and the fact that it cannot even come close to supplying our current energy requirements.

For example. Scotland announced that they were going totally "green" by building huge wind farms to supply all of Scotland's electricity. They closed coal-fired power stations and the coal mines that supplied them only to find that the wind did not blow often enough and so now keep two coal-fired power stations on permanent stand-by and have had to re-open several mines. This means that the pollution caused by the power stations is worse that it was before as the furnaces do not become hot enough to burn off the pollutants.

There is a huge lie about climate change (see later) and population increase which all connects in with the alleged short supply of food and fuels. We do have a changing climate – it is part of our consciousness change – but we do *not* have a growing population and the reasons for food shortages is the taking of productive land to grow bio-fuel crops and GM crops as well as the unbelievable amount of food wasted by western cultures.

According to "official" figures the world population is just below the seven billion mark. These official figures are based on an assumption that someone is born every second somewhere in the world so the totals just keep on rising. What the official figures do not do is take into account the number of people who are dying.

According to the Akashic, the world population peaked in 1996 at 7.4 billion. Since then, it has dropped radically and, at the start of 2011, the true world population figure stands at about 3.8 billion and is continuing to fall.

Climate Change

Throughout this book, I have tried to make note of the average global temperatures at times of change on the planet. This is to try to highlight the fact that whilst the world is warming up, the reasons for it are not man-made.

To start with, let us look at what is meant by average global temperatures.

We have a planet with two poles and an equator. The temperatures at the poles can plunge down to minus 60 degrees centigrade whilst the equator can have temperatures of up to plus 80 degrees centigrade. The high temperature equatorial air will tend to move towards the poles in a natural process. The temperature of the whole planet will be the average value between the extreme high at the equator and the extreme lows at the poles – this is what is meant by average global temperatures.

The temperature at the poles and at the equator is governed by the amount of energy produced by the sun. The average figure is surprisingly small; the highest it has ever been is below plus seven degrees centigrade and the lowest no more than minus three degrees centigrade.

If you look at the graph in Illustration Six you will see how the average temperature of the Earth has changed over the last one thousand years. These are official figures from the Metrological Office.

If we go back further in time than is shown on the graph to the time of Atlantis (85,000 to 65,000 years ago), the average temperature was at around plus 6 degrees C. This is borne out by archaeological findings that the south of Britain had rhinoceros roaming savannah grasslands at the time.

At the end of Atlantis, the destruction of the continent sent global temperatures haywire but even with it triggering an "ice age" the average temperature did not drop below minus 2.5 deg. C.

When we "returned" to Earth, 20,000 years ago, the average temperature was about 4 to 4.5 deg C.

Since then it has varied and these variations are to do with a combination of the activity of the sun and the consciousness levels of the planet.

It is known that 2,000 years ago the average temperature was around plus 4 deg C. This is confirmed by written accounts by the Romans who grew grape vines along Hadrian's Wall, on the English/Scottish borders, which produced "a very drinkable wine".

The temperatures dropped a little after this period but rose again. By about the year 1000, we entered what historians call "The Medieval Warm Period" where the temperatures were at about plus 2.5 deg C. This average temperature continued until about the year 1400 where temperatures began to drop sharply until, in 1480, the average global temperature dropped below zero and we entered a period known as "The Mini Ice Age". For almost 400 years, the average global temperature stayed at about minus 1.5 deg C.

As far as Europe was concerned, the Mini Ice Age was disastrous. It could snow at virtually any time of the year – there are written reports of snowfall in Kent in July – and so crops failed. Failing crops also led to a huge drop in population from starvation and disease with the main cause of death being "the Ague" (pronounced aagew), the common name for malaria. This was also the period of winter "fayres" on the Thames in London as the river froze for several months of the year.

The last Thames winter fayre was held in 1850 as this was the year that average global temperatures rose above freezing, signifying the end of the mini ice age.

So why do we think that climate change is man-made?

There is a document called "The Report From Iron Mountain" published in 1964 by a group who call themselves "The Council of Rome". This council is made up of members of deposed European royal families who support the New World Order as a means of regaining their old power-bases. In this document they propose that people are made to believe that the change in climate is man-made and that a "carbon tax" be imposed as a means of financing the New World Order.

Since the publication of this document, there has been a growing movement to persuade people that climate change is man-made – or

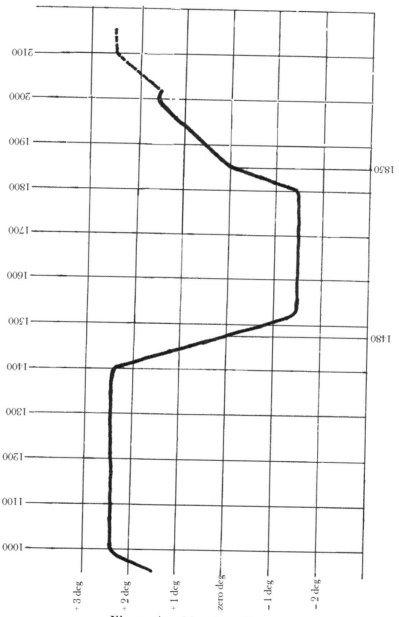

Illustration Number Six
Climate Change Over 1,000 Years

"anthropogenic" as many are now starting to call it. The "conspiracy" was laid bare by the release of the emails from the University of East Anglia's climate study department in early 2010 where thousands of emails were accidentally released showing that scientists had deliberately lied over the causes of climate change.

The biggest proponent of this "lie" has been the American politician Al Gore through his film *"An Inconvenient Truth"*. This film won Al Gore a Nobel Prize and an Oscar and is shown in schools all over the world to teach children about climate change. Except...

Having watched the film, a parent in the south of England decided to investigate the claims made. Following his research, he sued his children's Education Authority for teaching inaccurate material and the case went all the way to the British High Court. The court case was defended by the government's experts on climate change. The court case was based on 26 points made in Al Gore's film which the parent found to be inaccurate and, for reasons of their own, in 2009 the High Court only ruled on nine of these points. The ruling was:

The Court found that the film was misleading in nine respects and that the Guidance Notes drafted by the Education Secretary's advisors served only to exacerbate the political propaganda in the film.

In order for the film to be shown, the Government must first amend their Guidance Notes to Teachers to make clear that:

1.) The Film is a political work and promotes only one side of the argument.

2.) If teachers present the Film without making this plain they may be in breach of section 406 of the Education Act 1996 and guilty of political indoctrination.

3.) Nine inaccuracies have to be specifically drawn to the attention of school children.

The inaccuracies are:

1. The film claims that melting snows on Mount Kilimanjaro is evidence of global warming. The Government's expert was forced to concede that this is not correct.

2. The film suggests that evidence from ice cores proves that rising CO_2 causes temperature increases over 650,000 years. The Court found that the film was misleading: over that period the rises in CO_2 lagged behind the temperature rises by 800-2000 years.

3. The film uses emotive images of Hurricane Katrina and suggests that this has been caused by global warming. The Government's expert had to accept that it was "not possible" to attribute one-off events to global warming.

4. The film shows the drying up of Lake Chad and claims that this was caused by global warming. The Government's expert had to accept that this was not the case.

5. The film claims that a study showed that polar bears had drowned due to disappearing arctic ice. It turned out that Mr Gore had misread the study: in fact four polar bears drowned and this was because of a particularly violent storm.

6. The film threatens that global warming could stop the Gulf Stream throwing Europe into an ice age: the Claimant's evidence was that this was a scientific impossibility.

7. The film blames global warming for species losses including coral reef bleaching. The Government could not find any evidence to support this claim.

8. The film suggests that sea levels could rise by 7 m causing the displacement of millions of people. In fact the evidence is that sea levels are expected to rise by about 40 cm over the next hundred years and that there is no such threat of massive migration.

9. The film claims that rising sea levels has caused the evacuation of certain Pacific islands to New Zealand. The Government was unable to substantiate this and the Court observed that this appears to be a false claim.

Also, the Court's ruling included the following:

1. The film suggests that the Greenland ice covering could melt causing sea levels to rise dangerously. The evidence is that Greenland will not melt for millennia.

2. The film suggests that the Antarctic ice covering is melting, the evidence was that it is in fact increasing.

As you can see, the evidence presented by the film and the various governments that support the film, is fundamentally flawed and amounts to propaganda that cannot be substantiated.

It should also be noted that prior to making his film, Al Gore and his business partners set up a new bank which trades in carbon futures. As a result of his world-wide tour publicising his film, Al Gore and his business partners are all now multi-billionaires.

The truth is that global average temperatures are rising but they are rising because both humans and the Earth need them to. As we undergo our shift in consciousness, we need the temperatures to be higher to help in our development.

We also need there to be higher concentrations of carbon dioxide in the atmosphere. A high level of carbon dioxide helps the brain to function at its higher levels; if we kept the carbon dioxide levels low, it would slow down our ability to re-merge the soul into the body.

Take a look at point two in the ruling above: Carbon dioxide (CO_2) does not cause temperatures to rise – temperature rise increases the concentration of CO_2 in the atmosphere. So as the temperatures increase, so do CO_2 concentrations.

The current argument that CO_2 causes temperature rise is clearly false. The official argument being that temperatures have risen since 1850 because of the increase in CO_2 caused by the Industrial Revolution.

As can be seen from the graph, 1850 marks the end of the mini-ice age. In other words, temperatures were already rising naturally and were not man-made.

Neither is the CO_2 we produce making much difference to anything. Official figures are that man's activities produce 25 million tonnes of CO_2 annually and this is causing global warming. What the official figures do not tell you is that the Earth produces about 900 million tonnes of CO_2 per year. In other words, the Earth produces 36 times more CO_2 than humans every year.

The CO_2 produced by the Earth comes from earth fissures, earthquakes, volcanoes and decaying vegetation. This is one of the reasons for the huge increase in earthquakes since 1996: the Earth is putting more and more CO_2 into the atmosphere to help us undergo our change in consciousness.

The reality is that the temperatures began rising in about 1820, passing zero in 1850. The temperature continued to rise until 1995 where they peaked at about plus 1.5 deg C. Since 2000, the average global temperature has actually dropped – not by much, only fractions of one degree C – and not continued to rise. However, the activity of the sun has been very low since about 2000 – what is called a "Maunder Minimum" – but, at the beginning of 2011 activity began to increase again and we should begin to see global average temperatures rising again through 2011, 2012 and onwards.

I do not know what the average temperature is set to rise to yet but it will probably be no more then about 3 degrees C for the foreseeable future.

Remember, at the time of Atlantis, when we had our full soul within the body, the average temperature was plus 6 degrees centigrade.

The purpose of looking at the issues discussed in this chapter is to point out that we are being deliberately misled into believing events that are totally untrue. These deliberate lies are being made to distract us from our true purpose and fulfilling our true potential.

There are many reasons for these lies (see *Project Human Extinction*) but, what is important to remember is that if you have chosen to undergo our current shift in consciousness then what you need to do for yourself is paramount otherwise you will get left behind.

This means ignoring what is happening in the world, to a greater extent, as the energies for change are exposing all of the corruption and lies that have underlain our society for centuries.

As we progress through 2011 and 2012, the world is going to become much worse – try not to become distracted from your true purpose.

Chapter Thirteen

Religion

So we arrive at Chapter Thirteen.

Thirteen is an interesting number. For most, 13 means unlucky, especially if the thirteenth of the month coincides with a Friday – the reason for this is that on Friday 13th of October 1307, the French King, Philippe 1V, with the Vatican's backing, tried to destroy the original Knights Templar and the date has stuck in our collective memories.

But the number 13 was "unlucky" *before* that date as the Vatican tried to hide its significance from the population and made discussion of it a sin. This "sin" seems a little strange to me as, after all, Jesus the Christ had twelve disciples and 12 + 1 = 13. So the whole basis of the Christian church is based on the number 13 – does this make Christianity itself a "sin" in the eyes of the Vatican, I wonder?

The truth of it is that the number 13 is the Universal whole number; everything seems to add up to 13 in the end. The Creator intends to Create 13 universes, our Universe is protected and balanced by 13 beings and our Universe contains 13 races. So 13 really does count for something.

If I had to answer the question: do I have any religious beliefs? I would have to say no. If I had to answer the question: do I have a religion? I would have to say Animist.

An Animist is someone who can see the "spirit", or soul, at work in all things. As a psychic, I "see" the energies at work within all that there is, whether that is a living thing or the solar system or the Universe beyond. All are souls and all express their soul energies in different ways.

But, as we undergo our process of change, we are all beginning to see our place within Creation in slightly different ways and the traditional religious beliefs are becoming less and less tenable.

The rise of religious fundamentalism is a reflection that those who have religious beliefs are beginning to feel a little insecure within their traditional beliefs or at least insecure within the ways in which these traditional religions have modified their belief practices - the return to the original beliefs that brought that particular religion about.

So let us exercise a little fundamentalism of our own and look at how religious concepts and beliefs began.

The Origin of Religions
We looked at the nature of the Creator in Chapter Two and how the Universe is constructed around the energies of freedom of choice.

The Creator has Thought into Being all that there is; given the scale of the Creationery source, is it reasonable to assume that such a Being would require worship? I think not – especially as imbuing the souls of this Universe with the requirement that we "worship" our maker would negate our freedom of choice – if we choose to worship a deity, that is fine but demanding that we worship our Creator removes our ability to choose.

If you look at the way in which the six non-physical races and the seven semi-physical races lead their lives, you will find that they acknowledge the role that the Creator has played in bringing their existence into being but do not have any religious-type constructs around their understanding.

It therefore follows that religion, and the want to worship, is a man-made concept and, historically, this concept did not begin to arise until about 4,000 years ago.

We saw in Chapter Ten that the knowledge of how to use the Great Pyramid to re-merge the soul back into the body became the origin of a "Priesthood". However, the Priesthood was not formed for religious purposes but to be a group of people who would learn the secrets of the

Great Pyramid and allow others to make use of their knowledge if they required.

Nobody in ancient Egypt saw this knowledge as being of a "religious" nature. After all, if it is natural for you to see the spirits, souls, of other beings on Earth or in the cosmos, you would not turn it into a religion but accept life as it is in reality.

This changed when, 7,000 years ago, we adopted The Human Plan and reduced the amount of soul energy that was contained within the physical body - we literally became smaller within ourselves. But even this did not make us look for a "God" outside of ourselves.

There are also a great many misinterpretations of the past. Archaeologists have traditionally avoided making any interpretation of any spiritual or religious artefacts they uncovered as they felt that religion should be left to the Church. However, some archaeologists did begin to look at these spiritual artefacts in more recent years and it became the wide-spread practice to label anything that they did not understand as being "some kind of religious object" and ignored it.

This has led to a great many misunderstandings and misinterpretations of archaeological finds and given a much distorted view of ancient religious beliefs.

To find an understanding of how human religious beliefs came into being, we need to look to The Old Testament.

This "Book" is a collection of stories and recollections of one group of people who travelled from "Eden" to Egypt to Palestine and recent archaeological findings can help us to understand, more accurately what the story is about.

A great deal of The Old Testament deals with the life of Abraham and his descendants and he is seen as being the "father" of the three main religions – Judaism, Christianity and Islam.

Abraham originates in the city of Ur of the Chaldes which is located on the borders of current day northern Iraq and Iran, southern Turkey and Turkistan. About three kilometres from Ur of the Chaldes, is an ancient site known as Göbekli Tepe which has been under archaeological excavation since 1995.

The archaeologists have dated this site as being between 12,000 and 14,000 years old making it the oldest man-made structure on the planet. The Akashic dates it to more around 6,000 years ago.

Göbekli Tepe is a collection of underground buildings made from shaped granite "columns". Findings at this site have given an entirely new interpretation to the story of Abraham.

The original name for this region is Eden and the inhabitants are hunter gatherers who are fairly short in stature, dark haired and olive skinned. Their region is invaded by a group of people who came from "the north".

These northerners are very much taller than the locals and have white skins (tall white Nordics). These invaders are very strong and charismatic as well as being very aggressive. After conquering the locals, the northerners enslave them and insist that they are known as "gods". The local traditions also gives them various names including "Nephilim" and "Watchers".

These northerners have large skulls and almond shaped eyes which slope in towards the nose, giving them a bird-like appearance. Their traditions and shamanic practices centre around birds, particularly eagles and vultures with their main symbol being that of a disc with eagle's wings – a "winged disc".

These "Tall White Nordics" mate with the local women who produce hybrid children – the "gods came to Earth and mated with human women" - the origin of the "adamu" in the Annunaki fantasy story – and insisted that the first-born child be sacrificed to the gods and the infant children are placed in preserving jars – which has given rise to the local beliefs to become known as "Children of the Jars".

The northern gods force the locals into moving away from their hunter-gatherer lifestyles and become farmers in order for them to feed their "gods".

Eventually, the local people rise up, under the leadership of Yezidi, and massacre the northerners. Following this massacre, they leave Eden and travel south into Egypt taking with them their stories of their vengeful "Gods" who made them sacrifice their first born children to prove their love of their god.

Those of you who are familiar with the story of the Annunaki that has been translated by Zecharia Sitchin will no doubt find many parallels with the Annunaki fantasy (see *The Annunaki Plan?* or *The Human Plan?*).

Obviously, these findings place an entirely different slant on the origins of The Old Testament and, not surprisingly, have been labelled "heresy" by religious leaders.

The Meaning of Hell

Have you ever wondered how the concept of "burning in the fires of Hell" originated?

This, again, is connected with the peoples who left Eden and took their practices of sacrificing their first born child to prove their faith in God.

About 3 miles outside of Jerusalem is a valley called, in Hebrew, Ben-Hinnom or Ben-Gehenna. The Canaanite's name for the valley translates as "Hell". It is also known as "The Valley of the Shadow of Death".

This valley is narrow and slopes down from a plateau to the plain below. In this valley was located a very tall granite statue of the Canaanite demon God known as Moloch. In the centre of the statue was a brass bowl.

In order to practice the sacrifice of their first born child, the people went into the valley, placed their child into the brass bowl on the statue and lit a fire underneath. In order to drown out the screams of the dying child, priests were lined along the walls of the valley who beat upon huge drums.

This is the origin of the concept that demons control Hell and that the wicked will burn in the fires – it has, of course, become further embellished over the centuries but the images conjured up by what went on in this valley gives me the horrors.

There is also a greater irony here. At the bottom of this valley are a large number of tombs cut into the limestone walls – all of these tombs date back to about the year zero. In other words, to about the time of Jesus the Christ.

The burial practices at the time were that the deceased was wrapped in a shroud and placed on a shelf within the tomb. A stone was then rolled over the tomb's entrance and the body was allowed to decompose for about six months. At the end of this period, the tomb was re-opened and the bones collected and placed in an ossuary.

An ossuary is a box, usually made of stone, into which the bones were stored and, very often, the ossuary contained the bones of a number of members of the same family.

In the 1980's, an ossuary was found in these tombs which bore all of the names of Jesus the Christ's family. There has been great controversy over this ossuary as the inscription implies that the bones of Jesus the Christ, his parents and brothers and sisters are all contained within the stone box. Scientifically, there appears to be nothing incongruous about this ossuary, everything about it is consistent with a date of 2,000 years ago.

The ossuary and its contents are still subject to great debate but, if proven true, it means that Jesus the Christ and his family were buried under Hell.

Religious Wars

Having studied many aspects of most religions for many years, I have been struck by the contradictions of the concept of God. On the one hand we have a vengeful God whilst on the other we have a God who promotes peace. Both versions of God are accepted, seemingly without acknowledging the contradiction involved.

So, which is correct? Is the human God vengeful or is "He" peaceful?

There are a number of ancient cultures that are described as Pantheistic - this means that they worshipped multiple gods. I believe that these cultures were not Pantheistic but Animistic. In other words, they could see spirits, or souls, all around them and portrayed them in various ways within their culture. Modern-day archaeologists have interpreted these portrayals as being of multiple "gods" and not spirits who inhabit different realms.

The point is that if there were two Pantheistic cultures living next to each other, they led peaceful and peaceable lives. Contrast that state of being with two adjoining cultures who were Monotheistic – believed in one "God".

It is an historical fact that more people have been killed in wars between two, or more, Monotheistic nations than have been killed for any other cause. The most bizarre fact about these "holy wars" is that the believers fighting each other believe in the same God, it is just the way in which they practice their devotions that cause the problems.

The most horrendous example of this type of war was the Albigensian Crusade carried out by the Vatican against the Cathars in the first quarter of the 13th Century.

The Cathars lived in the Languedoc region of southern France and were a very peaceful people who believed in equality of all religions and full rights for women within their society. The Vatican decided that their views were heretical and massacred an estimated one million people during this crusade.

The Cathars did not kill people; they did not fight wars their only crime was to have a belief system that the Vatican did not like. The total world population at the time was an estimated 360 million so massacring one million Cathars killed out a sizeable proportion of the entire population. To put the figures into context; the current world population (official figures) is close to 7,000,000,000 (7 billion) one 360th of this figure is 19.5 million. So if the Albigensian Crusade took place now, the death toll would be in the region of nineteen and a half million people. All this because "my God is better than your God".

Manipulation of Religious Beliefs

The most obvious current use of religious differences is the western campaign against those who are followers of Islam – Moslems.

We are being propagandised into believing that all Moslems are potential terrorists and cannot be trusted.

We saw in the last Chapter that the campaign of terrorism aimed at western countries is actually fomented by the security agencies of western governments to keep their populations in a constant state of fear whilst fulfilling a secret agenda. Given that western countries are predominantly Christian; this campaign against Moslems could be seen as a "Holy War" or "Jihad" - as Moslems would call it.

My own experience of meeting those who are Moslem is that they are gentle, open-minded and friendly people who are utterly horrified at being placed in a state of mistrust especially as this mistrust is being deliberately engineered by politicians.

Talking of manipulation.

By a piece of interesting synchronicity, I was sent the email below as I was typing up this Chapter. It is reproduced here exactly as I received it – including the spelling mistakes and grammatical errors.

A Return is Requested....You'll See Why
Breakfast at McDonald's
This is a good story and its true, please read it all the way through until the end! (after the story, there are some interesting facts!):
I am a mother of three (age 14, 12, 3) and have nearly completed my college degree.
The last class I had to take was Sociology.
The teacher was absolutely inspiring with qualities that I wish every human being had been graced with.
Her last project of the term was called, 'Smile.'
The class was asked to go out and smile at three people and document their reactions.
I am a very friendly person and always smile at everyone and say hello anyway. So I thought this would be apiece of cake, Literally.
Soon after we were assigned the project, my husband, youngest son, and I went out to McDonald's one crisp March morning.
It was just our way of sharing Special playtime with our son.
We were standing in line, waiting to be served, when all of a sudden everyone around us began to back away, and then my husband did.
I did not move an inch...An overwhelming feeling of panic welled up

inside of me as I turned to see why they had moved.
As I turned around I smelled a horrible 'dirty body' smell, and there standing behind me were two poor homeless men.
As I looked down at the short gentleman, close to me, he was 'Smiling.'
His beautiful sky blue eyes were full of God's Light as he searched for acceptance.....
He said, 'Good day' as he counted out the few coins he had been clutching..
The second man fumbled with his hands as he stood behind his friend, I realized the second man was mentally challenged and the blue-eyed man was his salvation.
I held my tears as I stood there with them.
The young lady at the counter asked him what they wanted...
He said, 'Coffee is all miss' because that was all they could afford. (If they wanted to sit in the restaurant and warm up, they had to buy something. He just wanted to be warm).
Then I really felt it – the compulsion was so great I almost reached out and embraced the little man with blue eyes.
That is when I noticed all eyes in the Restaurant were set on me, judging my every action.
I smiled and asked the young lady behind the counter to give me two more breakfast meals on a separate tray..
I then walked around the corner to the table that the men had chosen as a resting spot. I put the tray on the table and laid my hand on the blue-eyed gentleman's cold hand.
He looked up at me, with tears in his eyes, and said, 'Thank you.'
I leaned over, began to pat his hand and said, 'I did not do this for you. God is working here through me to give you hope.'
I started to cry as I walked away to join my husband and son...When I sat down my husband smiled at me and said, 'That is why God gave you to me, Honey, to give me hope...
We held hands for a moment at that time, we knew that only because of the Grace that we had been given were we able to give.
We are not church goers, but we are believers.
That day showed me the Light of God's sweet love.
I returned to college, on the last evening of class, with this story in hand.
I turned in 'my project' and the instructor read it.
Then she looked up at me and said, 'Can I share this?'
I slowly nodded as she got the attention of the class.

She began to read and that is when I knew that we as human beings
and being part of God share this need to heal people and to be
healed.
In my own way I had touched the people at McDonald's, my son, the
instructor, and every soul that shared the classroom on the last night
I spent as a college student.
I graduated with one of the biggest lessons I would ever learn:
UNCONDITIONAL ACCEPTANCE
Much love and compassion is sent to each and every person who may
read this and learn how to
LOVE PEOPLE AND USE THINGS –
NOT LOVE THINGS AND USE PEOPLE.
There is an Angel sent to watch over you..
In order for her to work, you must pass this on to the people you
want watched over..
An Angel wrote:
Many people will walk in and out of your life, but only true friends will
leave footprints in your heart.
To handle yourself, use your head..
To handle others, use your heart.
God gives every bird it's food, but He does not throw it into its nest.
Send it back, you'll see why!
A box of gold
With a secret inside
that has never been told
This box is priceless
but as I see
The treasure inside is
precious to me
Today I share this
treasure with thee
It's the treasure of
friendship you've
given me
If this comes back to you
then you'll have a friend
for life but, if this
becomes deleted, you are
not a friend.
Send this to everyone you
consider a friend!
It will grant you one wish and only one wish,

that is, if you decide to send this to others. You can wish for anything.
Repeat your wish until you have finished scrolling..Make it count!
FOR YOUR WISH TO COME TRUE YOU HAVE TO SEND IT TO:
3 PEOPLE – YOUR WISH WILL COME TRUE EVENTUALLY
5 PEOPLE – YOUR WISH WILL COME TRUE IN 3 MONTHS
10 PEOPLE – YOUR WISH WILL COME TRUE IN 5 WEEKS
15 PEOPLE – YOUR WISH WILL COME TRUE IN 1 WEEK
CAN'T WAIT A WEEK???
22 people – Your Wish Will
Come True in 1 Day!
REMEMBER
THIS MUST BE SENT OUT THE
DAY YOU READ IT FOR
YOU TO GET YOUR WISH

The first time you read it, you think it is just a story of "Christian Charity" that is meant to make us feel good. But, if you read it again, a different message emerges. What it is saying is that if you believe in God, you do not need to go to church on a Sunday, you can go into a McDonald's hamburger restaurant at any time and still find Him - or maybe a sky blue eyed 'Saviour'. Does this mean Ronald McDonald is now going to dress up as Jesus?

Then when you read right at the bottom of the email you find that it is a piece of advertising sent out by Microsoft presumably on behalf of McDonald's:

Close ad
- ©2011 Microsoft
- Terms   Help Center
- Privacy   Feedback
- About our ads   English
- Advertise

If you follow the advice and send the email out to everyone on your mailing list; you are helping McDonald's to advertise for free.

But more than that, the "true" story engenders an emotional response which is connected in to religious beliefs. It also seems to imply that if we do not mirror the actions of the woman in the story we are not "Christian minded". Then there is the implied threat built into the story

– if you do not send it on to all of your friends you are a bad person who is without friends and is unloved. The advert also makes me despair that most people are desperate enough to send this on without reading it properly. It clearly states that it is an advertisement and yet I suspect that most would not have read that far before automatically sending it on without thinking about it first.

It is also a perfect example of the level of cynicism in the world where a hamburger restaurant considers itself a substitute for going to church.

I think I will stick to my Animist beliefs!

Chapter Fourteen

The Future

To quote the opening Chapter of *The Fool's First Steps*:

"It is the beginning of the twenty first century and we have walked a long and tortuous path to arrive at this time.

Gone are the builders of the pyramids, in all of their lands, and with them those who could understand their meaning. We stand on a radioactive refuse heap of our own making. The planet has reached the point where we are no longer able to undo the damage we have created. The pall of death and destruction pervades our every breath and our vision is clogged by the smoke from a thousand funeral pyres. The seas are throwing up their poisoned dead for our final inspection mourned by the echoes of the whales' song.

Such is the view of the world held by many.

But yet.

It is the beginning of the twenty first century and we have walked a long and tortuous path to arrive at this time.

The pyramid builders are returning. The crown chakra has begun to open and make our consciousness complete. The land has begun to swallow our mistakes and is helping to rebuild what once was. The death of many species has been overtaken by the re-emergence of the extinct. The fires of destruction lead to new growth and the seas bring forth their dead for us to grieve for our mistakes whilst harbouring new life and new growth in their hidden depths.

Such is the view of our world held by many.

We have arrived, but for the moment we are not sure where our journeyings have brought us. Our arrival on new old shores has, temporarily, made us lost."

I appreciate that this is a bit new-agey lyrical but it is the closest I am ever likely to get to writing poetry.

But the message is still the same: a proportion of the population see the world as being a "glass half empty" whilst the rest see a "glass half full".

We are standing on new old shores as we have arrived at the time in our history where we can return to the state of once more being a true Human Being – the way we were on Atlantis.

We have made a mess of our Mother Earth but She is doing everything She can to help us through our transition. Once through our transition, we will then be in a position to help Her in return and clear out the horrendous mess we have made.

The problem is that what we are doing on Earth has never been attempted before. Nobody, throughout the whole of Creation has ever undergone the trials, failures and successes that have occurred here on Earth. Is it any surprise that most of us are feeling excited and apprehensive at the same time?

As the energies continue to rise (see Illustration One), your higher self is attempting to find ways of bringing itself back into the physical body. As this happens, any emotional "debris" that you have hanging around your body will come under pressure to be cleared. So, for some, this time of transition will be a traumatic time. I have included exercises and meditations in the appendices which will help you sort these kinds of problems out. There are also meditations to help you connect more closely with your higher self as well as to explore some further answers for yourself.

The important thing to remember is: *do not panic!*
There is still time to resolve everything you need to resolve.

The Future

This book is being written in early 2011 and is intended to put our collective past into perspective so that, as memories of your past emerge as part of this change, you have a framework into which these memories can be placed.

Quite naturally, we all have misgivings about what is to come – this is the problem with the unknown.

So what is our future?

To be honest, there does not seem to be any accurate way of predicting just what is going to happen in 2012, 2013 and beyond, certainly not up to about 2050.

We are caught in the middle: how we change, how we cope with the change and just how much of our current life-styles will we need to let go of as we progress. We are used to living in houses with electricity, water and sewage connected which provide us with convenience at the flick of switch or the turning on of a tap – how much of this will we be prepared to let go of?

We are used to televisions, newspapers, mobile phones and the internet – what do we do if those are not there – especially when all of the satellites that make these things function are blown out of space by sun-spot activity?

If we re-merge the soul back into the body, how quickly will our higher psychic capabilities begin to function so that we do not need any of the above?

How will I personally know that I have changed? And how will I know when other people have changed?

These are the kinds of questions that many people are asking at the moment.

Then there is the question of what happens to those who have chosen not to go through with this change? After all, only about one third of the current population has chosen to progress in this way.

The Akashic does not have any answers, it records events as they occur, it does not predict the future.

But, we are not entirely without clues.

At the start of 2011, the number of people who had completed their process of reintegration was in the region of 4.3 million spread out over the globe. The vast majority of these Humans live in isolated tribal cultures and so did not have the trappings of the western world to hold them back.

However, there is one large group in Europe who have also undergone their early transitions. I am not going to tell you where they are as they have chosen to remain hidden. Even if you did go looking for them you would not find them as they have built impenetrable psychic barriers around the region where they live. But, I can tell you a little about how they have adjusted to their new lives.

This community is made up of about 400 men, women and children living in a region that has always been quite isolated from the outside world. As such, they do not have the millstones of western culture to let go of.

They do not use electricity or telephones of any kind and take water from wells or from streams which they psychically protect from pollution. Their food requirements are very low and, what they do need, they grow for themselves in ground they have psychically cleared of all pollutants.

They continue to live in houses but this is more for convenience than for necessity. They have also developed ways of keeping pollution out of the atmosphere around their region. Again, this has been achieved by psychic means.

In essence, the region in which they live has not changed a great deal to how it was before. Some of the people living there were local but a large proportion lived in other countries and in other cultures before their need to change attracted them to this region.

So this is a group of people drawn from many different cultures and who had many different religious beliefs. All live in harmony as they can readily see the soul underneath the skin colour and their need for religion has gone. No conflicts and no sense of competition – just the harmony of many souls working and "being" together in a common cause.

There, that doesn't sound too bad does it?

But, to be realistic, for those of us who live in westernised cultures, there is likely to be a great many more sources of conflict.

In recent years we have seen the massive rise of western imperialism and with it virtually complete removal of most of our personal freedoms. Anyone can be investigated by one government agency or another without our knowledge, virtually every town or city street has cameras that can recognise any face, every new car on the road can be tracked and immobilised by satellite and children can be removed from their parents without any recourse to appeal. Our governments ignore their electorate and carry out atrocities without any fear of reprisal from anybody. This is current western culture.

Our biggest problem is going to be how to undergo our soul re-merging with western culture doing everything it can to slow us down if not actually trying to stop the whole process. And to that, there is no immediate answer.

The start of 2011 brought with it mass peaceful demonstrations in several countries. Some of the country's leaders saw the writing on the wall and left peacefully whilst others ordered their troops to shoot the demonstrators. As we become more aware of our true selves, there is likely to be a want for a backlash against our western oppressive regimes but this will only play into their hands and put into force many of the hundreds of new laws that have been quietly passed in recent years to bring about marshal law and then we will have no freedom at all.

So the answer is not to take to the streets and revolt. The only real answer is to go within the self, to clear out our own personal problems and go with this change in consciousness levels. We will have to adopt an attitude of ignoring what else is happening around us and concentrate on helping ourselves and those who are changing with us and leave the rest of the population to sort its own mess out.

This is not being selfish; it is being realistic about what this new energy is bringing about.

We have changed very little over the past seven thousand years as we have been exploring our place within our world and learning how to overcome the problems we encountered first on Atlantis and then from 20,000 years ago.

Each successive life we have lived has seen us returning, time and time again, to the same kinds of problems we failed to resolve in previous lives. By constantly re-visiting these problems, we began to perpetuate a culture where we kept repeating the same mistakes. It was not helped by the fact that there were people who made use of the Fourteenth Faction energies that they had been contaminated with. Nor was it helped by the kinds of interference made by the Velon.

But, we always had choice. We either fought against them or, more often than not, we chose to do nothing, hoping that someone else would do it for us. This state of apathy has allowed those who wanted to take control to do so and we have ended up with all of the problems briefly mentioned above.

This situation is now changing and changing at an increasingly rapid pace. The first beginnings of change occurred in 1996 with the connection of new energy frequencies to the Earth which began this whole process of change. Since 1996, there has been increasing pressure on those who choose to change to sort out their lives but there has also been the start of a determined effort by those who do not want change to occur (Velon/Illuminati/Bilderbergers/governments etc – see *Project Human Extinction*) and this is why western laws have become more and more restrictive and oppressive and the reason why government agencies have been instilling fear into the population by blowing up their own citizens.

This is what I have been trying to say in this book: we need to stand back and see the bigger picture rather than becoming bogged down in the day to day detail.

The energy acceleration that began in November 2010 is becoming more and more difficult to resist especially since we started on the upward curve on the graph in Illustration One. This final acceleration began on the 29th of January 2011 and it made the pressure for change irresistible.

We are already seeing the effects of this acceleration in the street riots in several countries; as we continue onwards to December 2012, these energies have the potential to rip apart everything that stands in the way of our soul re-integration and so we will be faced with a world tearing itself apart at the seams. If you become bogged down in the ensuing mêlée, you will lose your chance to complete this change.

Another major factor to be taken into account is who has and who has not chosen to undergo this process of re-merging the soul back into the body.

There have been two major polls taken, one in September 1996 and the other in February 2005 where every single soul, connected with Earth, was asked one simple question – are you ready to undergo this process of change? This question was asked on a higher self level.

In 1996, the response was that 60 per cent of the then population was not ready; 40 per cent felt that they were. In 2005, the same question was asked but the answer was a little different: 65 per cent said they were not ready meaning those who said that they were had reduced down to 35 per cent.

Since the first census, the population has been dropping radically. From a high of around 7.4 billion in 1996, the total world population has, at the start of 2011, dropped to around 3.8 billion and is continuing to fall. Yet, despite a virtual halving of the world's population, most have not noticed or even continue to believe that we have a rising population.

Given that 65 per cent of the population has chosen not to go through with these changes, it means that they will have to leave the planet at some time in the near future. By that I mean that they will have to leave their bodies behind – die – and return to their place of soul origin.

Just how these people die will also be a matter of their own choosing. Some will just give up and not wake up in the morning; some will succumb to a fatal disease whilst others will use the method of their dying to help others to understand some of the problems that need to be resolved. For example: thousands of farmers in India are dying by drinking herbicides to highlight the plight of growing GM crops; people are dying in conflicts to free their country from a tyrannical ruler – deaths for this reason are likely to continue to grow as we have seen from the start of 2011 and there will be many other methods of dying that will be the choice of the individual.

Everything is choice and we are all free to make whatever choices we desire. The thing to remember is that none of these deaths are necessary: everyone on the planet has the opportunity to stay and undergo this change it is their own choice not to. Nobody is standing in judgement; nobody is saying you are a bad person and must leave; nobody is saying you worship the wrong God; all have free choice and all are freely exercising the choice they have made.

It is important to remember this over the next few years – it is free choice and only free choice that determines whether you stay or not – nobody is judging you.

The Near Future

This is why it is so difficult to predict what is going to happen over the next few years; but this is the most likely scenario in the short term:
- There will be a great deal of trauma as the old regimes collapse.
- There will be a large number of deaths as those who have chosen not to stay fulfil those choices.
- There will be disruption to how we currently live our lives as those who try to maintain the past are forced into letting go.
- There will be confusion and fear.

Despite all of this, there will be many millions of people who complete the process of re-merging the soul back into the body.

The problem is that it is impossible to predict with any accuracy the time scale over which all of this will happen.
It could all happen before the end of 2012; in which case, the trauma will be very severe but short lived.
Or, it could be that those who have chosen to leave are allowed to live out their natural life span. In which case the process could be extended over the next 50 years with our new lives finding a gradual balance but with the traumas of change, whilst not as acute, extending over a much longer period.

This is the problem with unique situations: nobody knows exactly how it will work.
But, from 2050 onwards, we will be on the road to a paradise regained.

The Mid-Term Future

I think we would all agree that we have made a huge mess of the planet. Since the start of the Industrial Revolution we have treated the planet as a source of raw materials and little else. Certainly we have not behaved as though we were staying.

We seem to have lost sight of the fact that we are living on, and being supported by, a lump of rock floating in space. We have nothing else. As human beings, we have nowhere else to go. Yet look at the destruction we have wrought all because we have been brainwashed into believing that we need more material goods and we have fallen for it.

The war in the Darfour region of the Congo is not, as we have been led to believe, a war between rival war lords but is being sponsored by western countries to gain control over mineral rights in the Congo Mountains. The main mineral of interest is called "coltan" (columbite/tantalite) which is essential to the electronics industry. Flat screen TV's, lap top computers and, most of all, mobile phones all need this mineral to operate at the speeds we now demand of them. We are literally killing millions of people just so you can carry your Blackberry.

This is the ruthlessness depicted in the film *"Avatar"* but happening in real life and we are closing our eyes to it just so long as we have the latest mobile phone.

So at some time in the near future, we need to fulfil our contract with the Earth and begin to clean up our mess.

It is only after we have completed our re-integration process that we can begin to carry out this clean up work. By 2050, at the latest, we will be able to do the job properly. We can only effectively sort these problems out when we have regained our full psychic potential. Then, and only then, will we be able to understand what we are doing and to be of effective help to the planet.

Pollution free seas, pollution free skies and pollution free land are all achievable – once we have our full level of understanding and capabilities.

Once that work is complete, we will return the Earth to the paradise that She truly was and we will be able to live our lives as they are meant to be lived – as they were lived on Atlantis.

So take responsibility for your life and your actions and do it.

I wish you all a safe journey.

Appendix One

Thirteen Most Asked Questions

When I used to wander about a bit and give talks, people would always ask me questions. The questions rarely varied as people tend to share similar concerns.

So, set out below are the thirteen questions I was most asked together with a brief answer for each. Obviously, if you would like a longer answer, all I can suggest is that you read my books – see the end pages of this book.

Q1. Who am I and where do I come from?

A.   You are a soul, an immense consciousness that has chosen to come to Earth and build for yourself a human body in order to discover how physical life is lived.

There are two possible types of soul origin. The first accounts for over 99 per cent of humans and that is the six "non-physical" races who most people would consider to be "Angels". The second possible soul origin is that of being from one of the "semi-physical" races. This soul origin accounts for les than 1 per cent of the human population. See Chapters two and Three.

Q2. Are "Angels" (the non-physical races) higher beings than those of the semi-physical races?

A.   Only a human would ask this question – nobody else throughout the Universe would even consider that there could be a difference. All souls are Created and there is no "higher" or "lower" – just souls.

Q3. (a) What am I doing here?
    (b) I have a sense of having a job to do. What is it?

A. (a) Like all other humans, you have come to Earth to experience physical life on a planet where the experience is unique. For the last 7,000 years, we have, collectively, been exploring how we find our way to re-merging the whole of the soul back into the physical body.

(b)   The feeling of "having a job to do" is very common amongst those who are currently physical. Essentially, we all have a role to play in the same "job"; that is to complete our individual part of The Human Plan and put our collective knowledge to work so that as many people as possible can re-merge the soul back into the body.

Q4. (a) How old is my soul?
    (b) What does it mean when mediums tell me that I am an "old soul"?

A. (a) If you are of the non-physical races soul origin; you will be 100 million years old. If you are of the semi-physical races soul origin, you will be 30 million years old.

(b)   As you can see, there are only two possible ages for your soul and neither of these ages makes you new or old on a soul level. The term "old soul" usually applies to someone who has more experience or wisdom from living numerous human lifetimes. It usually means that you seem more relaxed about life than most, nothing more.

Q5. I was told that new souls used to be born to close-knit tribal communities so they could be taught how to be human – is this correct?

A.   This is either a misunderstanding or wishful thinking. If we had all lived our first human lifetime with a traditional tribal community learning how to live on the Earth, I think that we would be considerably more environmentally aware and not have allowed the destruction of the planet.

Q6. What is a chakra?

A.   There are seven primary energy centres within the body (see Illustration Five) all located along the spine between the top of the head and the very base of the spine commonly known as chakras. The word chakra is originally Sanskrit and means something like "spinning wheel of light" which describes what the chakras actually look like when viewed from the front. When viewed from the side a chakra looks like a cone of energy.

Each chakra is an aspect of the soul made physical and is one of the ways in which our higher self communicates to the physical aspect of the soul.

Q7. (a) How do I know what lessons my soul wants me to learn?
    (b) How do I know when I have learned it?

A.   If you keep asking the question "Why do I keep finding myself in the same situation?" it is because you are not learning what your higher self wants you to learn and is repeatedly putting you back into similar situations until you break the cycle.

The main way in which the soul (higher self) communicates to us is through the chakras. If our chakras are fully open and fully energised then we are doing what our soul wants us to. But, if we go against the soul's wishes, we deplete the energy of one, or more, chakras and we develop symptoms of illness. This is what an illness is – the soul trying to tell us that we have strayed from our chosen path.

(b)   We know we have learned our lessons when we stop recycling in the same or similar situations and our lives become less complicated.
In addition, we know when we have learned the lessons our soul wants us to when the symptoms of illness we have been experiencing have disappeared. If we are not listening to the soul, the symptoms of illness become more intense until we do pay attention to what our soul is trying to tell us. Death is the ultimate message from the soul to tell us that we have gone very wrong in our lives. But at least on death, we can work it out and build for ourselves a new body and try again.

Q8. (a) Does the planet have a soul?
     (b) Do animals have souls?

A.   Yes, the planet is an immense consciousness (soul) who has created all plant and animal life and works very closely with each and every human. The way in which we stay on the planet is through our first (root) chakra which connects our soul to the planet's soul – it isn't gravity that keeps us on Earth but our soul to soul connection to the planet.

(b)   Animals are a little different to humans in that they do not have individual souls. Animals have a group soul – for example: a group soul for elephants, a group soul for bears or a group soul for dogs. Each animal is an individual but, for their whole lifetime, they remain connected into their group soul and return to their group soul on death. Animals such as cats and dogs also have group souls but when they are connected with particular people as pets or companions, they can draw more energy from their group soul and make them more of an individual but still connected to their group soul.

Q9. When you die, who is it that meets you?

A.   In the vast majority of cases the one that greets you on death is your higher self. However, the souls of people you were particularly close to in the life you have just left can also be there to greet you and lead you to your higher self.

Q10. How quickly after death can you reincarnate?

A.   The period between lives can vary considerably. On average, it takes about one hundred years to plan out your next lifetime. However, it is possible to plan to start a new life even before you leave the last one. This is possible by reducing the amount of soul energy you keep in your current body – for example someone who is in a coma or someone who has dementia can reduce their level of soul energy out of one body and transfer it into a new-born child. The choices and possibilities are as individual as the soul.

Q11. Why can't I see the Faerie?

A.   It could be as simple as the Faerie do not want to see you! Generally speaking, it is usually inappropriate for people to see the Faerie for two reasons. The first is that if you could see the Faerie, you would be tempted to spend all of your time with them and would not get on with the things your soul wants you to explore in this particular lifetime. Secondly, there would be the temptation to shout your ability from the rooftops which would only get you locked up and so you still wouldn't do what your soul wants you to.
The real answer is that if it is appropriate for you to work with the Faerie then you will do so. If your soul does not consider it

appropriate then no amount of wishful thinking will make it happen. When you have completed your soul reintegration, you will be able to see the Faerie quite naturally.

Q12. Can anyone access the Akashic?

A.   Yes, anyone can access the Akashic; but, it requires an open mind, practice and discipline. It also requires that your higher self thinks it is a good idea – see Appendix Five.

Q13. If several million people have already completed their soul re-integration, why are they not helping everyone else to complete?

A.   Every single soul connected with Earth has the absolute freedom of choice to choose their actions and so each individual, who is currently on Earth, has chosen whether they are going to complete their part of The Human Plan or not. In order to complete our soul re-merging, we need to take actions which clear out the debris we have accumulated during our lives. If you have chosen to go through with your own soul reintegration then you need to clear out the emotional debris you have accumulated through this lifetime. It is obviously your choice as to whether you achieve your own clearance – nobody can do this for you. So the reason why those who have completed their soul reintegration are keeping themselves hidden is that there is nothing they can do to help you until you have helped yourself.

The other reason why they remain hidden is that the rest of the population would turn them into the "Meritrea" or the "Second Coming". This would not be very helpful at this time as it would distract people away from their own path to clearance and reintegration.

Only you can complete your own soul reintegration, nobody can do it for you.

Appendix Two

Chronological Chart

14,376,279,393 years ago	Creation of Universal envelope
100 million years ago	Creation of the six non-physical races
40 million years ago	Completion of our solar system with early life beginning to form on most of the planets
30 million years ago	Creation of the seven semi-physical races
25 million years ago	Earth began to explore the possibilities offered by physical forms of life
20 million years ago	Creation of the Sidhé and the Faerie
4.5 million years ago	Neanderthal Man developed by the Earth from early proto-humans
4 million years ago	The arrival of the planetary Guardians

3.9 million years ago	Four of the original thirteen planets in our solar system choose to remove themselves from the physical "experiment". The debris of two of these planets forming the asteroid belt between Mars and Jupiter and Earth's Moon. The remains of the other two planets are just outside of our solar system giving rise to the idea of Planet "X" – the tenth planet or possibly now known as Tyche.
3.8 million years ago	The adoption, by the Earth, of the Cro-Magnon Man template from Mars. Virtually all life was instantly destroyed on Mars by the destruction and removal of the four planets. Earth adopted Cro-Magnon as a possible additional development to Her Neanderthal.
3.6 million years ago	The Fourteenth Faction broke into this Universe in search of raw resources resulting in the contamination of the energies of freedom of choice.
94-98 thousand years ago	Period when Lemuria was established on an ice island in the southern Atlantic.

85 thousand years ago	Atlantis established – see Illustration Four
65 thousand years ago	Atlantis destroyed
65 thousand years ago	Construction of the Sphinx in Egypt as a marker for the entrance to the principle underground "shelter" used by those who stayed on Earth to help rebuild the damage caused by destroying Atlantis. Other shelters exist in South America, entrance near to Teotihuacan and in Britain, entrance under West Kennet Long Barrow.
28 thousand years ago	New energy matrix constructed around the planet to support the shortly to arrive new human population. The energy matrix is more commonly called the "Ley Line Grid".
20 thousand years ago	Six regions of the Earth were re-colonised by souls from each of the thirteen soul origins. Each colonised region began to explore our connections to the Earth. The full soul Human template was adopted as the "standard model" for the Human body.

18 thousand years ago	Construction of the Great Pyramid – sometimes called Khufu or Cheops Pyramid. The original concept was that only this pyramid was required to fulfil its psychic reconstruction role. As humans became more and more "physical", the other pyramids were added until, about 15,000 years ago, all seven principle pyramids were complete. These seven pyramids, the central three at Giza with the other four at locations matching the stars of the Orion constellation, were designed to connect together into a massive energy collection and focussing structure – see *The Universal Soul*.
17 thousand years ago	Construction of the pyramids at the other colonised sites except for Britain.
16 thousand years ago	Adoption of sexual reproduction. Although the "normal" conception and birth process had been experimented with, all new lives were brought about by "Adult Birth" up until this time. Sexual reproduction was not fully adopted by everyone until 7,000 years ago.

12 thousand years ago	First use of a written language based on the electrical impulses that run along the spine. This "binary" language became the root of all written languages.
10 thousand years ago	The first phase of the construction of Stonehenge.
8 thousand years ago	The majority of people leave the planet to merge with their higher self to discuss the way forward for Human life on Earth. This "discussion" led to the formulation of "The Human Plan".
7 thousand years ago	The beginning of The Human Plan being put into action. The human template now becomes divided into two – the "physical self" and the "higher self". The Human Plan meant that everyone designed a series of lifetimes in order to gain as much knowledge as possible of how to be human on Earth and to regain the original Human template of the whole soul within the physical body. This knowledge gathering process has become known as "Karma". The Earth has considered people to be "sub-human" ever since. In agreement with the Earth's consciousness,

we imposed a 7,000 year time limit which expires at the end of 2011.

1 thousand years ago

The Velon race discovers the primary energy flow to our solar system – see *Project Human Extinction.*

Recent Chronology

August 14th 1996
17.30 BST

The connection of the new energy grid to north Devon. The new energy overlays and reconstructs the old Ley Line Grid constructed 28,000 years ago. The new grid activated the twelve global primary energy points – see *The Journey Home.* Connection of the grid triggers the first census of human readiness for our completion process.

December 31st 1999

Start of the acceleration of the human energy structures allowing further choice and actions. These energies reached their peak at the end of May 2003. With this peak, the process of change became unstoppable and could not be reversed.

30th May 2000	The Earth alters Her base-note frequency from 7.56 Hz to 3.5 kHz. The frequency of the root chakra of all living things, including humans, now resonates at the new frequency changing the colour of the root chakra from red to copper gold – see *The Universal Soul*.
June 2nd 2003	The first people to complete the whole soul reintegration process – 25 in the USA and 43 in Europe. Several million have joined them since.
1st August 2004	The Earth confirms that the original Atlantean Human template is the only acceptable Human form. No other versions of humanity will be allowed on the planet after 2011.
2nd August 2004	The Earth charges up all global crystal deposits that remain in the ground.
February 2005	As energies settled and reinforced, a second census was taken of human readiness to complete their part of The Human Plan. These new energies brought about a further increase in the death rate and a slowing of the birth rate.

November 2010	The start of the final energy acceleration which will raise all frequencies to 3.5 kHz as a minimum frequency.
January 29th 2011	The rising energy frequencies begun in November start their final acceleration.
November 2011	Finish of the final acceleration of energies begun in November 2010. This act of completion will allow all of the people who have chosen to undergo their soul reintegration to do so.
2012 and onwards	There is no map available to help us arrive at our destination. This new part of the Human experiment will unfold as we pass through it. This does mean that we can actively construct our own future without constraints or limits but there are likely to be many problems we will need to overcome before we finally get there.

I Wish You All A Safe Journey!

Appendix Three

Chakra Meditation

The idea of this meditation is to fully energise and balance all of the chakras. By working in the way described in this meditation, there is no need to "shut down" afterwards as your energy fields will be virtually impenetrable to outside influences.

Always insist that you are working directly with your higher self and that there are no other "beings" trying to work through you.

Remember that the chakras take the form of a vortex. This is a little like an ice-cream cone with the point attached to the spine with the "bell" of the cone opening outwards, away from the body – see Illustration Five. All of the chakras have increased in energy and so they are all of the same energy form, they no longer need any colour. The chakras look a little like the 'heat haze' shimmer you see on a hot day – totally transparent shimmering energy. This is the energy that all of the chakras are now formed from. It does not matter which direction the chakras spin in – what feels right for you will be right for you, just follow your intuition.

Start by using your usual method of reaching a state of relaxation. Once you are relaxed and in a meditative state, begin to form a point of concentration about 30 cm (one foot) above the top of your head.

Once you feel your concentration has formed a small ball, bring this point of concentration all of the way down the spine to the first (root) chakra. When you have reached the very bottom of your coccyx, form the cone pointing directly downwards with the point attached to the bottom of the coccyx. The cone of energy is totally transparent 'heat haze' with no colours. Try to make the cone spin as fast as possible. The faster it spins, the more transparent it becomes, the more transparent, the faster it spins. When you feel you have achieved this, move up to the second chakra.

The second (sacral) chakra is located just where the spine meets the pelvis. This time, there are two vortices, one attached to the back of the spine and one attached to the front. Both of the cones of energy open equally front and back. Try to make these cones spin as fast as possible using totally transparent energy. The faster they spin, the more transparent they become, the more transparent they become, the faster they spin. Once you have achieved this, move on to the third chakra.

The third (solar plexus) chakra is located on the spine about 2.5 cm (one inch) above the tummy button. Again, there are two vortices, both opening equally front and back. Try to make both cones spin as fast as possible using totally transparent energy. The faster they spin, the more transparent they become, the more transparent they become, the faster they spin. Once you have achieved this, move onto the fourth chakra.

The fourth (heart) chakra is located on the spine at the level of the heart. Again, there are two vortices, both opening equally front and back. Try to make both cones spin as fast as possible using totally transparent energy. The faster they spin, the more transparent they become, the more transparent they become, the faster they spin. Once you have achieved this, move onto the fifth chakra.

The fifth (throat) chakra is located mid way between the Adams apple and the chin. Again, there are two vortices, both opening equally front and back. Try to make both cones spin as fast as possible using totally transparent energy. The faster they spin, the more transparent they become, the more transparent they become, the faster they spin. Once you have achieved this, move onto the sixth chakra.

The sixth (third eye) chakra is located on a line with the spine just above the bridge of the nose. Again, there are two vortices, both opening equally front and back. Try to make both cones spin as fast as possible using totally transparent energy. The faster they spin, the more transparent they become, the more transparent they become, the faster they spin. Once you have achieved this, move onto the seventh chakra.

The seventh (crown) chakra is located at the top of the head and opens directly upwards on a line with the spine. The point of the cone is on the top of the head with the cone opening directly upwards. Again, using totally transparent energy, make the cone spin as fast as possible making the energy as transparent as possible.

Once you have achieved this, bring the point of the vortex down the body, connecting into all of the chakras in turn. In other words, connect the seventh chakra to the sixth chakra then to the fifth then to the fourth then down to the third and then down to the second. Once you have connected the crown down to the first chakra, all of the chakras become fully balanced and fully energised.

Once you have done this, bring your point of concentration back up to the point you started with above your head and slowly bring yourself back to the present or move on to one of the other meditations.

Appendix Four

Higher Self Meditation

T he purpose of this meditation is to reinforce the connection between you and your higher self. Again, make clear your intent that you only wish to work with your higher self and *not* an outside entity.

Begin with the chakra balancing meditation. Once you have completed the full sequence of the meditation, bring your point of concentration back to just above the top of your head.

We are on the side of a mountain, very near the top and just climbing onto an open area, like a small plateau. The air is clear and fresh and we feel healthy and invigorated by the climb. We are comfortably warm, but not hot, and we are breathing easily after our climb.
As we step onto the plateau, we see lots of bushes with large silver flowers and, as we breathe in the musky perfume of these flowers, we feel a sense of achievement – we have at last reached the higher ground. We can turn back and look down on our climb and see that all of our struggles, exertions and fights are now far behind us. We no longer need to climb – we have arrived. As we look back on our climb, we can look back and see if there are any areas of our life which we have neglected and which require us to spend a little time to finally clear out.

Do not be afraid of these unresolved areas.

Remember, you are looking at your life and they are a part of you that needs a little effort to finally clear out. Do not ignore them. Remember them and realise that these small items are all that need to be resolved. All else has been cleared.

As we turn back to the plateau, we realise that our vision has changed. It is as if a mist, a veil, has cleared and we can see the peaks of other mountains around us and that they are all below us. We feel our sense of achievement, we have arrived and our world has changed because of our climb.

We find a comfortable spot to sit down on and enjoy this feeling of completion. Let us just savour this feeling for a moment. No more climbing to do, all we need to do now is just to be.

As we sit and relax, we become aware of an energy. It is as though we are being showered in a transparent sparkly light from a little way above us. As we become more aware of this energy, we become more aware of a mind within it. A mind that is sharing itself directly with our mind and we acknowledge that this mind is closely connected with us. A part of ourselves that is very familiar but somehow larger than us.

As this higher aspect of ourselves comes closer to us, connections begin to be made directly between our higher aspect and our physical aspect. We become aware of the long chords that have always connected the two aspects together and that these chords are becoming shorter and stronger and we feel that both aspects are beginning to merge into ourselves.

We can feel ourselves expanding. Our awareness fills a new larger space and we can see and sense the world in newer and fresher ways. We feel that we can at last understand ourselves and our world in new ways and with a new light of understanding.

We slowly, slowly return into the now with the sure knowledge that this expanded self of ours is firmly in place and fully connected, never again to be separate.

Slowly, we return into the now feeling relaxed, refreshed and all of our chakras fully balanced.

Appendix Five

Akashic Meditation

The purpose of this meditation is to bring yourself to the point where you are able to access the Akashic directly. However, working within the Akashic requires practice and discipline. In order to achieve this level of practice, it is best to make use of the following meditation in order to familiarise yourself with the methods of obtaining information. For most people, the following "Library" meditation is sufficient to answer all of the questions you might have. However, if your Higher Self agrees that you would benefit from accessing the Akashic directly, after you have practiced with this meditation sufficiently, your HS will open a door at the far end of the library through which lies the Akashic. Please note that this door will not appear until such time as your HS considers you are ready, and able, to deal with the experience.

Begin with the "Chakra Balancing" meditation and ensure that *there are no other "beings" trying to influence you.*
Once you have completed the full sequence of the meditation, bring your point of concentration back to just above the top of your head.

You are in a garden. It does not matter what type of garden it is: it can be formal, it can be wild or it can be woodland. It is your garden and can be constructed exactly the way you want it to be. You can spend as much time as you like in your garden but, at some point, allow yourself to focus on the house that is part of this landscape. This house needs to be huge, like a palace or a stately home and make your way slowly to the front door of this house. Once you have climbed up to the front door of the house, just push the front door open.

As the door opens, you can see a grand hallway. At the far left end of the hallway is a door – walk down the hall and open this new door.

In front of you is a library. This is why your house needs to be as large as you can imagine it because you could not fit this library into a house that was any smaller. The library is filled with books. The walls are lined with books from floor to ceiling and there are bookshelves sub-dividing the room which are also filled from floor to ceiling. The room always has enough light to be able to read any book no matter where you stand or sit within the library.

There are three ways to use this library. First, you can ask the library a specific question, it does not matter what kind of question it is, the library will present you with a book from which you can read the answer.

Secondly, you can ask the library if it could present you with something which will be of interest to you at this time. Again, the library will present you with a book from which you can read.

Thirdly, you can wander around the shelves and pick out books which catch your attention and you can read what your chosen book has to say.

There are probably many other ways in which the library can be used - these three are suggested in order to get you started on your search for answers. You can access the library for just about any information of any kind – just use as you choose. There is only one warning – it can be very tempting to spend a great deal of time in the library and the time outside will pass very quickly, so it is better if you set yourself a time limit before you enter it. Your mind will remember and bring you out of the library at the right time.

As the library begins to fade, bring your point of concentration back to above the top of your head with the knowledge that you will remember the information you gained at this particular visit.

Concentrate on your body and your chakras for a moment feeling that they are fully energised and balanced. Then, open your eyes and slowly return to your room and the present time.

Appendix Six

The Giveaway

Throughout our lives we find ourselves in situations where we feel we are unable to express ourselves as fully as we would like. This can be with members of the family, with friends or colleagues or with our employer. The problem is that all of the unexpressed emotions of these kinds of situations become lodged in our internal organs. If the emotional debris becomes too great, it can cause the organ to break down and generate symptoms of illness.

This has been bad enough in the past but, as we undergo our process of change, the storage of old emotions will actually hold us back if not actively prevent us from moving forwards. Obviously, these stored emotions need to be removed from our bodies.

The best way of clearing these emotions is to confront the person who brought about the emotions in the first place and express to them how you really feel.

If you are unable, for whatever reason, to do that, the next best way of clearing these stored emotions is with a process called "The Giveaway".

The Giveaway

The giveaway is a process of writing down all of the emotions that you have stored away. This sounds as though it cannot work – until you try it. What you will find is that once you start, all sorts of emotions and situations that you thought you had dealt with will come to the surface and you will realise that you are carrying a huge amount of emotion from your past.

For this exercise, you will need:

One old newspaper

Several pencils
One glass of organic red wine (optional)
One candle (optional)

The most important thing to remember about this exercise is that:
YOU DO NOT READ IT BACK.
The reason for this is that if you read back what you have written, you will take all of the emotions back in and have to start again.

This is the reason for the newspaper and the pencil; it is virtually impossible to read pencil on newsprint. It is also the reason for the candle; if you use this exercise in the evening with only candle-light, it makes it even more difficult to read.

The optional glass of organic red wine is included as it helps you to relax and allow your expression of held emotions to flow more freely.

So, find a quiet time in your day where you will not be disturbed. Collect your newspaper and pencils and sit down somewhere comfortable.

Think about something that has happened recently which made you upset but you could not express yourself fully. Using a pencil on the newspaper, start to write to the person who brought about the emotions. Write in whatever language you like – the stronger the language the better.

As you write, you will find that other emotions connected with other events come to the surface. That is fine, you can add those to what you are writing – just keep on going.

Once you have finished a session of writing, rip up the sheet of newspaper you have been writing on and dispose of it – burning it is best if you can. Don't worry if you cannot burn it, just rip it up into the smallest pieces you can and throw them in the rubbish.

You will need to do this exercise many, many times. This is not just a one-off exercise.

You will know when you have written enough about a particular situation when you are able to think back on the events and not feel any emotion at all. If you think back and still feel emotions rising up, you need to do another giveaway.

This exercise sounds far too simple to do you any good. Try it and you will find that a huge weight feels as though it is being lifted from you.

You can also write to inanimate objects that have caused you stress – such as broken pipes, a leaking fridge, traffic jambs, queues in the supermarket, etc. etc. It makes no difference what the situation is, write a letter to it and it will clear out the emotions.

Just remember DO NOT READ IT BACK or you will undo all of the work you have done in writing by taking all of the emotions back into the body.

This exercise works and works extremely well and will actively help you through your transition.

Best Of Luck!

Please Note: this exercise has to be written by hand – it cannot be done on a computer. If you try to use a computer, you will inevitably read it back off the screen making the exercise pointless!

Books by Chris Thomas
Published by Fortynine Publishing

The Annunaki Plan? or The Human Plan?

We are not a slave race.
Do we acknowledge the truth we know is within ourselves
or do we accept a different truth –
one which has been imposed upon us without our choosing?

The Human Plan
is a plan we wrote ourselves,
a plan which is reaching its long awaited conclusion
in 2011/2012

The Annunaki Plan
is the connecting force between the
Illuminati, the Bilderbergers, governments and Lucifer –
the "god" of the Freemasons.

Which Plan we choose to adopt – and we do still have time –
will determine the next 1,000 years of our history.

This book clarifies the choices – the choice is yours to make.

79 pages paperback   ISBN 978 - 9566696-0-5   UK price: £6.50

Fortynine Publishing
PO Box 49
Llandysul
SA 44 4YU

Fortynine
publishing

Interviews with Chris Thomas

Several interviews with the author are now available

See Chris Thomas on **YouTube**
in an interview with
Miles Johnston

Two interviews each lasting about one hour

Now available on DVD
To buy this DVD contact
eileen@gibson398.orangehome.co.uk

New DVD
An interview by Chris Thomas
With the international award winning film maker
Terje Toftenes

DVD lasts two hours and twenty minutes

DVD can be bought from:
Eileen Gibson
eileen@gibson398.orangehome.co.uk

Podcast Interview with Chris Thomas
Interview lasting approximately one hour
on

www.thespiritguides.co.uk

Books About Human History & Earth Mysteries

The Journey Home

We are Human

We bring together our inherent spiritual natures and dense physical bodies and try to make them fit. All of the difficulties that we have experienced through all of our many lifetimes have led us to create and perpetuate myths and mysteries that have only served to alienate and confuse us to a point where we have forgotten our true natures.

As we begin a new phase of human history and development, a new understanding is emerging which begins to break away from those who would keep our true place in the universe secret.

This book attempts to cut through the half truths and mysticism and put our history and state of being into plain language. Many of the answers to our age-old questions have been available since mankind appeared on Earth but, over the centuries, they have become hidden by personal interests and clouded by repetition and dogma.

104 pages paperback   ISBN 186163041-7   UK price: £7.95
Published by Capall Bann
www.capallbann.co.uk

The Fool's First Steps

It is the beginning of the twenty first century and we have walked a long and tortuous path to arrive at this time.

We have arrived, but for the moment, we are not sure where our journeying has brought us. Our arrival on new-old shores has, temporarily, made us lost.

As with the Fool of the Tarot cards, we have travelled full circle and are poised to start afresh.

This book takes the first few steps into a new understanding of many of the world's mysteries and begins to look outwards to other life on other worlds and how they have helped to shape our past and present.

We are not a body that has a soul but a soul, an immense eternal consciousness, which has built for itself a body.
We are starting to bring the body and the soul into an integrated one and realise that we are everything that we ever dreamed we are and considerably more.

178 pages paperback   ISBN 186163072-7   UK price: £9.95
Published by Capall Bann
www.capallbann.co.uk

Planet Earth - The Universe's Experiment

Who are we? Where do we come from? What is our purpose and why did it go so wrong?
Humans are not of the Earth but have arrived on this planet to explore. On our joyous arrival we encountered the spirits of the land – the Sidhé and the Faerie. As we became more human, we began to lose our memories of our origins and the knowledge of our true purpose and potential.
As we approach the completion of our climb back to reality, we are awakening to the ghosts of this knowledge.
Lemuria, Atlantis, the thirteen races have all played their part in "The Human Plan", all are now working to assist us to our chosen goal – full consciousness. But, time is short and unless we complete our journey soon, the Earth will be lost to us.
Virtually all of our experience and history is at odds with the scientific versions of our past, only the Akashic tells the real history. What is told here is the Akashic's story.

202 pages paperback   ISBN 186163 224 X   UK price: £11.95
Published by Capall Bann
www.capallbann.co.uk

The Universal Soul

Curiosity, this is how life begins.
A curiosity along the lines of "What If?" Together with the energy potential to imbue a lifeless void with the souls who are to explore the "what if" on behalf of the one who asked the question.

Our Universe explores the "what if "of freedom of choice. Every soul that exists within this Universe has the right to choose their own actions, their own directions. All choose freely without limitations.

The exploration of the physical has led to the existence of Earth and all of the life that our Earth supports – a miracle of creation and evolution.

There have been many trials and tribulations throughout our Universe and some of these events have brought the whole "thought" to a point of near destruction. One thing has sustained this Universe above all else – the Earth must be protected at virtually any cost.

With humanity finally finding the answers to a question we asked ourselves 20,000 years ago, we are entering a new phase of existence and this process has repercussions on the Universal whole.

192 pages paperback   ISBN 186163 273-8   UK price: £12.95
Published by Capall Bann
www.capallbann.co.uk

The Human Soul – Universal Soul 2

We live in troubled times which do not appear to be improving.

All of the promises of forward movement for the human race moving towards our completion appear to have ground to a halt. Not only halted but racing backwards to a point of self-destruction.

Our current state pushes us to look for answers, often without fully knowing what the questions are. But, the places we have traditionally looked towards to providing these answers are increasingly failing to give satisfaction.

The purpose of this book is to show why we are failing in our search for the truth. It also fully updates the problems generated by the race we know as the Velon under their more commonly known names of Hathor and Annunaki – their true story is not as they would have us believe.

By investigating these answers, both through the Akashic and published material, it is hoped to give enough information so that by gaining that knowledge and understanding, it will help you to take back your own power and achieve the longed for soul reintegration.

245 pages paperback   ISBN 1-86163-299-1   UK price: £13.95
Published by Capall Bann
www.capallbann.co.uk

Project Human Extinction - The Ultimate Conspiracy
By Chris Thomas with Dave Morgan

This is a book about power. The power to control the money supply, the power to control governments, the power to control multi-national business, the power to control the media, and above all, the power to prevent the identity of those in power from becoming known.

The ability to wield this power has become known as "The Conspiracy". This conspiracy has been at work for nearly 250 years and yet most are not even aware that it exists.

What this book does is to unlock the key secrets of the conspiracy and to identify the key players and the forces at work behind this power-base.

Many will find the findings shocking whilst others will have already arrived at a similar conclusion for themselves.

Whatever you thought was going on in the world is almost certainly wrong.

This book can help you to understand why you have been so powerless for so long.

390 pages paperback   ISBN 1-86163-312-2   UK price: £16.95
Published by Capall Bann
www.capallbann.co.uk

Books About Healing by
Chris Thomas & Diane Baker

Everything You Always Wanted to Know About Your Body But, So Far, Nobody's Been Able To Tell You

Have you ever wondered why some people become ill and not others?

Do you know how the body really works?

Why do diets rarely work?

Is there an alternative approach to treating illness instead of prescriptive drugs?

This book leads you through the body, organ by organ, system by system in simple language and clear illustrations.

It relates each organ to its associated chakra and explains how our day to day lives have an influence on our health.

It also takes a look at how illnesses are brought about by past life traumas.

It is a very comprehensive look at the body and illness and deals with illness at a root cause level. The second half of this book also contains a comprehensive guide to many alternative treatments for all symptoms of ill health.

456 pages paperback   ISBN 186163098-0   UK price: £17.95
Published by Capall Bann
www.capallbann.co.uk

The Sequel to Everything – The Case Histories

Although this is a sequel, it can be read independently as it explores how the body really functions by using genuine case histories taken from the authors' "psychic surgery" clients.

Forty six case histories are discussed to illustrate how the body is a function of, and directly controlled by, the soul.

Symptoms of illness arise because we have taken a step away from our soul's purpose. This book helps to bring back full health and accelerate full consciousness integration by helping you to understand the messages from the soul through the body.

This book further explores how past life choices can have a profound affect on our health in this lifetime, travelling as far back as Atlantis and beyond.

There is also a section exploring food additives and chemical toxicity.

202 pages paperback   ISBN 186163 1375   UK price: £11.95
Published by Capall Bann
www.capallbann.co.uk

The Healing Book

We are all Healers.

All that we need to do is to stop telling ourselves that we are not.

This book is for those who wish to heal. It starts at the beginning of the healing process with simple, easily followed exercises which can begin to unlock the healing potential which is inherent in all of us.

These methods apply equally to humans and to animals.

If you do not have any experience of giving healing, but would like to learn, this book can set you on that path.

If you already work as a healer and would like to explore your greater potential, this book is also for you.

The first half of this book is about learning to heal from the beginning. The second half begins to explore some of the energy manipulation techniques used by the authors in their daily practise as "psychic surgeons".

132 pages paperback   ISBN 186163053-0   UK price: £8.95
Published by Capall Bann
www.capallbann.co.uk

*Please note: The Healing Book makes mention of an audio tape to accompany the book. This tape is no longer available. The meditations detailed in the appendices have now superseded the meditations that were included on the tape.

To order **signed** or further copies of this book,

Synthesis

Please write to:

Fortynine Publishers
PO Box 49
Llandysul
SA44 4YU
Please include your email address

Costs UK: £9.50 per book postage and packing free

Rest of EU: £9.50 per book plus postage and packing of £2 per address
plus £1 per book (UK currency only)
Rest of the World: £9.50 per book plus postage and packing of £3 per
address plus £1 per book (UK currency only)

**Cheques or Postal Orders only and made payable to
Chris Thomas**

Cards NOT accepted at the above address

Note: We can only accept cheques in pounds sterling drawn on a
British Bank

Please allow 14 days for delivery

**All books and DVDs are also available from Cygnus Books
(cards accepted)**

www.cygnus-books.co.uk